EXCEL

2021

Everything you need to know about Excel
to go from Beginner to Expert

NORA E. WRIGHT

engaging in the rendering of legal, financial, medical or professional advice. The content within this book has been derived from various sources. Please consult a licensed professional before attempting any techniques outlined in this book.

By reading this document, the reader agrees that under no circumstances is the author responsible for any losses, direct or indirect, which are incurred as a result of the use of information contained within this document, including, but not limited to, errors, omissions, or inaccuracies.

TABLE OF CONTENTS

INTRODUCTION

Excel is a spreadsheet application and one of the most widely used PC programs in the world. It's simple and robust enough to track budgets and manage projects and secure and export data, all without any programming knowledge. It's also easy to use and can be accessed by everyone, whether their first language is English or not.

It may seem like an IT job that's too complicated for the average user to do, but Excel is designed to be easily learnt and, with the right training modules, may even be accessible enough for you to use without help if you want it. You can find corporate training courses in your area; see your local Microsoft office or consult the manuals. If you'd like a little more structure than these manuals offer though, you'll need much more than this one text.

Learning Excel is a fine choice for you if you're a good programmer and already have a lot of knowledge about spreadsheets. In this book, I'm going to provide details on the main areas that you'll need to know to become competent with Excel, from basic understanding to advanced features.

While many readers will be familiar with Microsoft Word for Windows and Outlook, a similarly versatile application is the PowerPivot add-in for Excel. It was developed by Microsoft as an alternative way of working with detailed data in Excel, and lets you work at a higher level of abstraction not possible using simple spreadsheet functions.

With so many alternatives available, why learn Excel? Well, let's have a quick look at the advantages and disadvantages of Excel to help you decide whether it's worth your time.

Excel is a great program for those who have to manage data collections, from sales figures to sports results or from employee data to house sales. It was originally developed as a software tool for businesses and now has many different uses. In fact, it has been widely used in education as well as manufacturing.

It is also excellent for those with time-limited projects or who would like something that makes sense when they are not an expert in the subject at hand.

Microsoft Excel is a spreadsheet software, a computer program for manipulating a large amount of data on a single sheet of paper. Spreadsheets can be used to present financial information, such as columnar income statements or summary income statements. They can also be used for payroll purposes, but they have several drawbacks compared to other types of spreadsheets:

There are several different ways to use Microsoft Excel. For example, the "traditional" way of using Excel is to access it through Excel Files. You can save all your work in an excel file and then open it again later by opening the file with the program you used to save it.

A common usage of Excel is to create a pivot table. A pivot table allows you to make calculations on the values in a column. For example, you can add up all the income from a column by using a sum function. Through the use of 'trim' functions, it is also possible to adjust data values correctly by correctly adjusting values for data combining it with other data. One of the most commonly used functions is "Sum" which subtracts all numbers or numbers of different categories from each other or sums all numbers after grouping them together.

This book will cover the most important concepts of Microsoft Excel from a beginner's point of view. Inside the book there are a series of examples with a clear explanation.

So, let us begin?

Getting Started

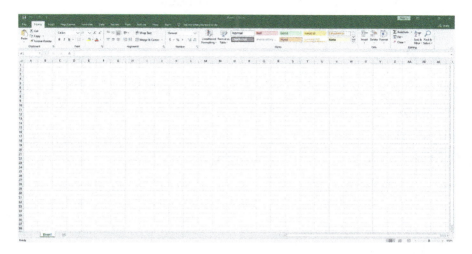

Before we start talking about complex formulas and functions, you need to start familiarizing yourself with the Excel work environment and a number of basic concepts. Here you'll learn everything you need to know about the user interface and all the elements surrounding Excel workbooks.

If you've already worked a bit with Excel and you know how to find your way around the environment, you could skip this. However, if you're new, or it's been a while since you last worked with this program, you should refresh your memory before continuing with the rest of the book.

Workbooks

Before we dig into the heart of the matter, you need to understand the hierarchy behind Excel. Here it is in a nutshell:

- The Excel programs
- The workbook
- The worksheet inside the workbook
- A given range within the worksheet
- The cell within the range

What we have here is called an object hierarchy. The Excel program holds the workbook objects, which in turn contain worksheets, that are made out of range objects made up from the final element, which is the humble cell. Microsoft refers to this hierarchy as the Excel object model. However, the main component we're interested in right now is the workbook. No matter what kind of operations we're performing in the program, they all take place inside the workbook.

On a side note, until the 2003 version, whenever we saved a workbook file, it had the .xls extension. Since Excel 2007, they will now be saved with an .xlsx extension. This is similar to Word 2003 having a .doc extension and the later versions having a .docx extension instead. Does the difference matter? To us, not really, unless you're trying to open a xlsx file using the pre-2007 versions, which you can't. The difference is that the xls file is a simple binary file that any Excel version can access. The newer xlsx files are compressed folders that contain all the files which hold data such as formatting, charts, and any information inside the cells.

There's no limit to how many workbooks you can create since each one is set in its own window; however, you can have only one active at a time. Sheets work the same with only one being active. You need to navigate to the bottom of the window where you see all of your sheets, and select the one you want to switch to. As an alternative you use keyboard shortcuts like Ctrl + PG UP to switch back to the preceding sheet or Ctrl + PG DN to activate the next sheet.

In order to rename the sheet, you can either double-click on the sheet tab or right-click on it to bring up a menu containing various options. Furthermore, you can choose to hide the active workbook window by navigating to the view tab, followed by the window tab, and click on the "Hide" option. Take note that you can view a workbook in multiple windows, thus allowing you to see a different sheet in each window and make your work a bit easier. You can go with this option by clicking on "New Window" in the Window tab.

The worksheet we keep referring to is the most common type of sheet, which is basically like any spreadsheet you find on other applications meant to work with tabular data. With that being said, working with multiple sheets doesn't mean working with more cells, because one single sheet can contain a massive number of cells that isn't even worth worrying about. The benefit of using several sheets revolves around organization.

If you work with a single sheet, you'll end up with a lot of different data that will take a lot of time to maintain. So instead, you can have a different sheet for each type of information. You can access any sheet instantly and manipulate it however you want because you can hide various columns, change the heights and widths of the rows, choose to have several lines inside the same cell, merge cells, and much more.

Furthermore, you can also create chart sheets instead of worksheets. Their purpose is to contain a chart. However, a lot of people don't use this type of sheet because they have the option to use an embedded chart which will appear inside the sheet's drawing layer. Therefore, you don't necessarily have to use chart sheets, though it would be easier to do so because it's easier to organize them and use them for presentations.

Any version of Excel that came after Excel 2007 allows you a great deal of customization, and they all work in nearly identical ways.

The User Interface

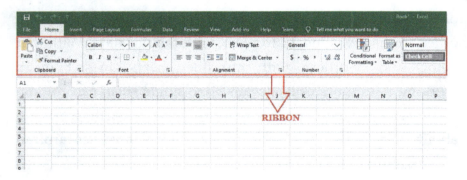

RIBBON

All programs have some way to communicate to the user, and that's through the user interface. Excel's UI is made up from the following components which we'll talk about in more detail:

- The Ribbon and Tabs.

- The Quick Access Toolbar.
- Shortcut menus that pop up when you right-click on an object.
- A mini toolbar.
- A number of dialog boxes.
- Task panes.
- Keyboard macros/shortcuts.

The ribbon is the main UI element because it provides us with a main area where we'll find all the commands we use most frequently. This allows us to work faster. Essentially, the ribbon is a collection of tools that are spread across the program's window. It also contains several tabs that are found in all Microsoft programs, such as Insert, Home, etc. Each one of these tabs contains the tools that are connected to the category. So, for instance, in the home tab we'll find a collection of Font options, Alignment commands, and much more.

We can customize the ribbon as we wish by resizing it or collapsing various tool sets and tabs to create a minimalistic setup. If you minimize the program, the ribbon's contents will be minimized automatically, and by default the maximized window will display everything you need. Take note that the tools will always be accessible even if not readily visible. You'll just need to go through some extra steps to get to them.

Finding your way around by using the ribbon is quite easy. You select a tab and then click on the tool you need. If you really want to master Excel and work really fast, you can learn how to use keyboard shortcuts instead of mouse clicks. You can look up and memorize them, or you can hold the Alt key and hover your mouse over each tool to reveal its shortcut. Learn as you go and soon enough, you'll be using more and more shortcuts, especially for those tools you use often.

For instance, if you hit Alt + HBB, you'll create a double border under whatever you selected. The Alt key is used to activate the shortcuts, then the H will select the home tab, while the first B navigates to the Borders menu where the second B initiates the command called "Bottom Double Border." Just don't forget to hold Alt down while you type the other shortcuts, otherwise this won't work.

Next up we have the contextual tabs that are contained within the ribbon. These tabs appear only when we access them particularly as they are usually hidden until we click on a certain object, such as a chart. A perfect example for this is the Drawing Tools tab. We need to click on a shape object to enable it as it contains a number of tools and options that can only be applied to shapes.

Now, if you navigate to the bottom of the ribbon groups, you'll see a little icon that stands for the dialog box launcher. This will launch a dialog box that's linked to a particular group, like the Font group. So, the Font group icon will launch a dialog box for formatting cells if we enable the font tab. The process is the same for other groups and dialog boxes. The Alignment group will launch the exact same dialog box as the font group, but it will enable the Alignment tab instead of the

Font tab. Take note however, that you won't be using these dialog boxes often because the ribbon remembers the most often used options and tools, and therefore you'll be accessing them from the ribbon.

Another collection of tools can be found in the form of a gallery. There are multiple galleries that represent certain categories, such as the Styles gallery which lists the style name and gives us an idea about the form of our object if we select it. This type of tool is extended with the Live Preview which allows us to display the data we select and see it as it will look once, we add it to the worksheet. All we need to do is hover the mouse over the chosen object. For instance, you can hover over the Format Table gallery and you'll see how the table might look like. This allows us to make a choice before fully committing to it.

Next, we have the File tab which is unique. When you click on it, you'll be taken to the Backstage View where you'll be able to perform a number of actions that are focused only on the document itself. For instance, you'll have the option to set up a new workbook, to save your files, to manage your printing, open other files, and more. In addition, the backstage view contains an Options dialog button that will launch a dialog box that contains a number of settings used to customize the Excel application.

Take note that next to all of these tabs and collections of tools we also have a number of shortcut menus that only appear once you right-click on a selected object. Therefore, these menus depend on the context. In Excel, you can pretty much right-click on any type of object and it will bring up a list of options that will only apply to it.

Finally, we have the dialog boxes that are displayed by certain ribbon commands. There you can go through various options and select other commands. Excel's dialog boxes can be divided into two different categories:

The modal dialog box: These boxes will have to close first before executing a chosen instruction. For instance, we have the Format Cells dialog boxes that work that way. Nothing will execute until you either click OK or the Cancel button to close the dialog box without confirming any commands.

The modal-less dialog box: They are the so-called "on top" dialog boxes, such as the Find and Replace option. The main difference is that they will always remain on the screen, and they're available no matter which other activity you're performing. Its modal counterpart requires user interaction before continuing with the execution and doesn't permit us to switch to other activities unless we confirm or cancel the action.

Customization

The first collection of tools you might want to customize is the Quick Access toolbar. Normally, after the installation, this toolbar will only contain the Save, Undo, and Redo options. So, if after working a bit with Excel you realize that you're using some other commands on a routine basis, you might want to add it to the toolbar. All you need to do is right-click on the command, usually a ribbon command, and select the "Add to Quick Access Toolbar" option from the menu.

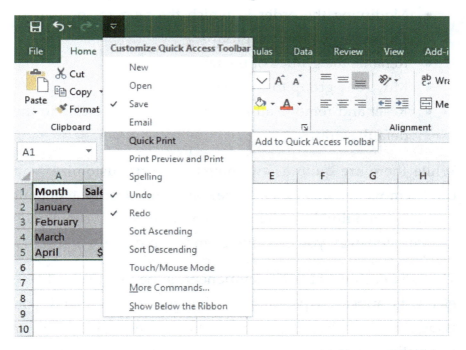

Other modifications can be made from the Options dialog box. To access it you need to right-click on the Quick Access toolbar and select the Customize option. You can customize the ribbon the same way by selecting the appropriate option in the Options dialog box. Remember that to access this dialog box you need to navigate to File and there you'll find a command called "Options."

Here are some customization options you'll have:

- Inserting a new tab.
- Adding a group to the tab.

- Inserting new commands to the group.
- Removing the commands from the group and the group from the tab.
- Modifying the order in which the tabs are presented. The same goes for the groups.
- Rename the groups or the tabs.
- Move any group to another tab.
- Reset and remove all modifications by reverting to the default settings.

While there are quite a few things you can customize, you can't remove the default tabs, the commands from the default groups, or modify the order in which those default commands appear. However, you can hide them if you'd like.

The next customizable UI component is the task pane. These elements appear depending on the type of command you issue. In essence, they're a form of response to your instructions. For instance, if you right-click on a picture, you can select the Format Picture option. As a response, the program will open the Format Picture pane. Task panes are in many ways identical to the dialog box except that they can remain visible for as long as you want and perform other tasks around them.

Normally, they will be docked on the right side of your screen, but you can move them by just clicking the title of a pane and dragging it elsewhere. Take note that this customization will be saved because Excel will remember where you placed a particular pane last, so when you open another Excel instance, the pane will be where you left it. You don't have to change its location whenever you run a new program.

Lastly, Excel allows you to modify certain onscreen elements like status bars and the ribbon. For instance, we can use the Ribbon Display options to instruct the program how to display the ribbon. We can choose to hide everything, minus the title bar for example. This way we declutter the window, which is a good thing if you're used to working with minimal user interfaces. Furthermore, we can change the status bar at the bottom by right-clicking it and choosing from a menu which type of data to display.

There are other customization options which you can explore on your own by heading to File and selecting Options. There you'll find an Advanced tab with a number of sections and commands related to customization. Try them out and forge the perfect UI.

Microsoft Excel Basics

The Excel User Experience

1-Quick Navigation:

You only need to press the Ctrl key next to any keyboard direction key, this will save you time if you want to go to the end of the sheet where there is data.

2-Composition of text in a single column:

Very similar to the CONCATENATE option, when you want to join in a single text several that are in separate columns, use the "&" symbol and press Enter. The structure will be (= cell1 & cell2 & cell3 ...)

3-Change from lowercase to uppercase:

When you have the lowercase text and want to convert it to uppercase, you must use the text format = SHIFT (cell) on the contrary if what you need is to pass it to lowercase, the format is = MINUSC (cell).

4-Identify duplicate information:

This trick is one of the favorites for those who must analyze a lot of data in a spreadsheet and it is very simple to find these duplicate content cells. The first thing you should do is select the column and select "conditional formatting" in the start bar, then "duplicate values" and then "enter".

5-Freeze column titles:

If your spreadsheet has more rows than what allows you to see your screen, you will necessarily have to scroll and many times you can forget in which column is the information you want to see. But this is solved if you select the row where the titles are, then go to the "view" tab and click freeze top row.

6-Create pivot tables:

We know that you are not yet an expert, but pivot tables are a great tool if you want to analyze and compare different types of information. The first thing you should do is to organize it in rows and columns, then select them and in the tab "tables" click on "pivot table" (make sure that each column has its header or title). A box will appear in which you can configure the information presented in the form of a table, by selecting and dragging with the mouse to each blank box you can organize it in a simple and very practical way.

7-Remove unnecessary spaces

When imputing formulas there is nothing that generates more stress than finding the word "Error" and not knowing where it comes from, many times the extra spaces are the cause of this alert and removing them is very simple! All you have to do is write the formula = SPACE (cell that contains the spaces).

What is the VLOOKUP Function?

The VLOOKUP function is an Excel tool that is used to locate a value within a specific date range. That is, with it you can determine immediately if in a table exists a value or not. It should be noted that this function is one of the most used in Excel, so it is essential to know how to use it.

The formula to use is: = VLOOKUP (search value, table array, column number, [range search])

Search value: is the value that is repeated in both tables, and which you want to identify. In this case, type «A» is searched, for this, the first value located in the table on the left side in cell C3 must be chosen.

Table array: corresponds to the range of the table located on the right side, in which the search will be performed. According to the example shown, this will be F3: G5, which should be set with "$" in case you want to drag the formula.

Column number: is the column number that is indicated to Excel, which contains the data that you want to obtain as a result. According to our example, this would be column 2 where the "description" information is shown. When the function finds a match of the search value it will show us, as a result, the information located in the column indicated in this argument.

Range search: FALSE will be used to make sure to match exact values.

It is recommended to ensure that at least one of the columns is repeated identically in both tables. To do this, check the data set to verify that the column of data that you will use to mix the information looks exactly the same, also taking into account the spacing.

Below are the most basic functions in the spreadsheet not only of the Excel program, specifically these are the functions that we will explain:

- Sum
- Subtraction
- Product
- Division
- Percentage
- Maximum and minimum
- Average

Basic Functions in Excel

Sum: With this function, what we calculate is the sum of all the numbers in a data set (also called range). It is represented in the Excel sheet:

= SUM (cell (s): cell (s))

Subtract: Analogously to the sum, but with the sign - instead of the sign: And it will be:

= REST (cell (s) -cell (s))

Product: Multiply all numbers obtaining the product of those numbers. It will appear:

= PRODUCT (cell (s); cell (s))

Division: Similar to the product. The formula will appear:

= DIVIDE ((cell (s)/cell (s))

Percentage (%): Excel calculates the percentage of a series of data, dividing the amount by the total. The expression of this function is

= PRODUCT (%; cell (s))

Maximum and Minimum: With this Excel function you will indicate the maximum and minimum value of a set of values. A) Yes:

= MAX (range) y = MIN (range)

Average: Returns the arithmetic mean of a series of values. With the expression:

= AVERAGE (range)

Exercise with functions in Excel

In the exercise that we explain below, you will perform your first actions to practice with Excel functions, suppose you have the following data:

Type in cell A1: figure 3 and in cell A2: write 2.

You are located in cell A3, you want to add these numbers, for this you will:

Insert, Function, choose Sum and click with the mouse or directly type in the first rectangle A1 and in the second A2 we accept, we get 5.

Proceed in the same way to calculate the rest of the functions explained and so you will have done your first steps in Excel.

Customizing Excel

To change text fonts, colors or general appearance of objects in all spreadsheets of the book quickly, try switching to another theme or customize a theme to meet your needs. If you like a specific topic, you can do it by default, all new books.

To switch to another topic, click Page Layout > themes and then select the one you want.

To customize that theme, you can change its colors, fonts and effects as necessary, save them with the current theme, and then make the default theme for all new books if you wish.

Change theme colors

Choosing a different theme color palette or changing its colors will affect the colors available in the color picker and the colors used in the book.

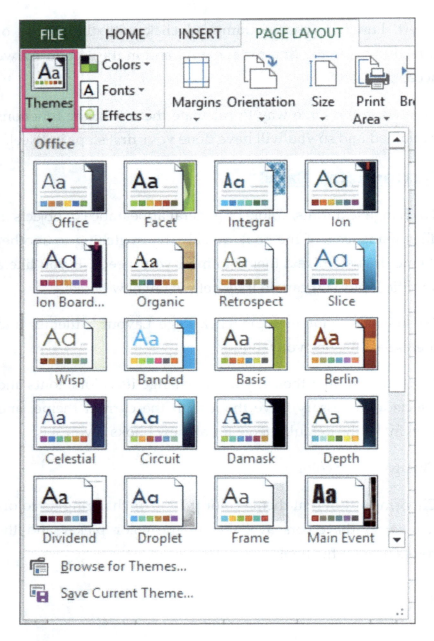

1. Click Page Layout> colors and then select the color set you want.

The first set of colors of the current theme is used.

2. To create your own color set, click Customize colors.

3. For each theme color you want to change, click the button next to color and choose a color in Theme Colors.

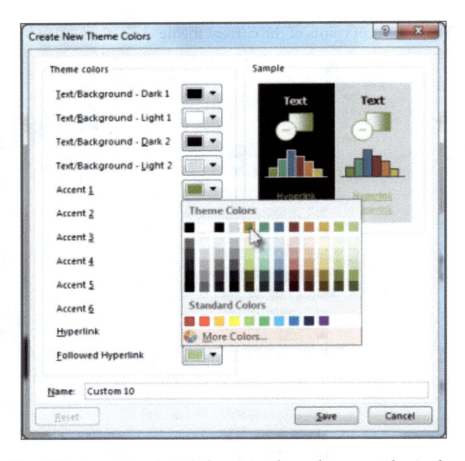

To add your own color, click more colors, choose a color in the standard tab or enter the numbers in the custom tab.

Trick: In the box shows, preview the changes made.

4. In the name box, type a name for the new color set and click Save.

Trick: You can click Reset before clicking Save if you want to return to the original colors.

5. To save the new theme colors with the current theme, click Page Layout> themes> Save Current Theme.

Change theme sources

Choosing a different theme font allows you to change the text at the same time. To make it work, make sure that the body and header fonts are used to format the text.

1. Click Page Layout> Fonts and then select the font set you want.

The first set of sources of the current theme is used.

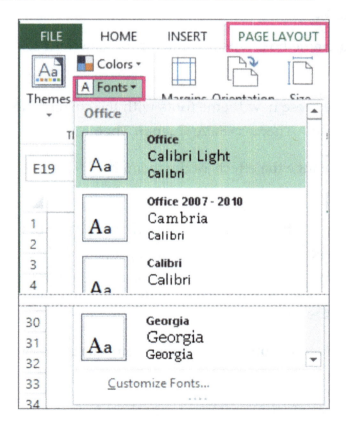

2. To create your own font set, click Customize fonts.

3. In the Create new theme fonts box, in the header font and body font boxes, select the fonts you want.

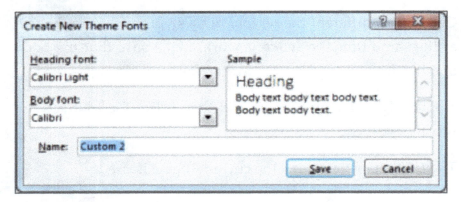

4. In the name box, type a name for the new font set and click Save.

5. To save these new theme fonts with the current theme, click Page Layout> Themes> Save Current Theme.

How to change the effects of the theme?

To reach that purpose, two main steps are important. Choosing a different set of effects changes the appearance of objects used in the spreadsheet by applying different types of borders and visual effects such as shading and shadows.

Here are the steps:

1. Click Page Layout> Effects and then select the set of affects you want.

The first set of effects of the current theme is used.

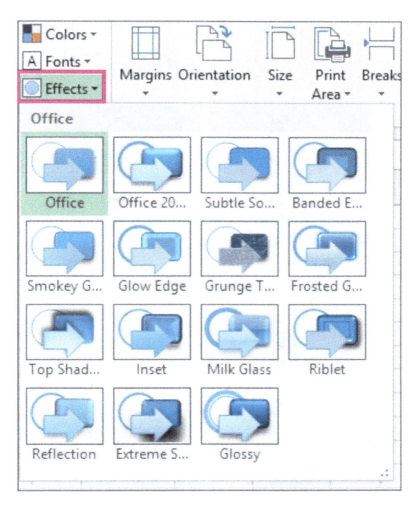

Note: You cannot customize an effect set.

2. To save the affects you have selected with the current theme, click Page Layout> Themes> Save Current Theme.

Save a custom theme for reuse

After making changes to the theme, you can save it for reuse.

1. Click Page Layout> Themes> Save Current Theme.

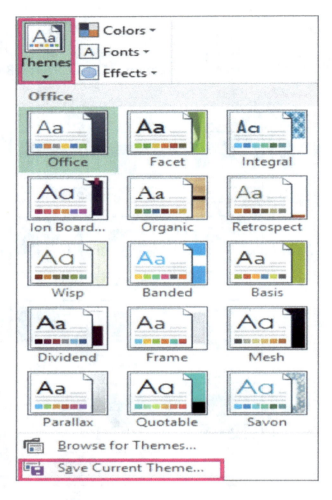

2. In the file name box, type a name for the theme and click Save.

Note: The theme is saved as a theme file (.thmx) in the document's theme folder on your local drive and is automatically added to the list of custom themes that appear when you click on themes.

Use a custom theme as the default value for new books

To use the custom theme for all new books, apply it to a blank book, and then save it as a template with the name book.xltx in the XLStart folder (usually C:\Users\username\AppData\Local\Microsoft\Excel\XLStart).

To configure Excel automatically open a new workbook using Book.xltx:

1. Click file> Options.

2. On the General tab, under Startup Options, uncheck the Show home screen when this application starts.

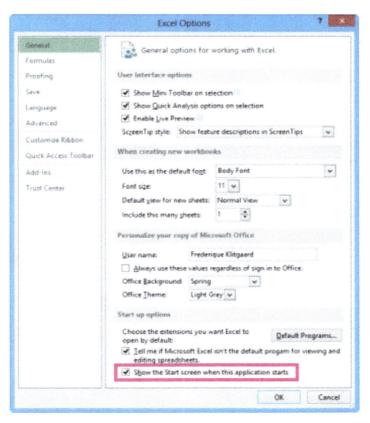

The next time you start Excel, a book that uses Book.xltx will open.

Tip: If you press Ctrl+N, you will create a new book that uses Book.xltx.

Basics of Excel Formulas

We are going to explore the basics behind working with Excel formulas. You'll learn how to enter and edit formulas, which operators to use and what they do, how to determine the cell and ranges used in formulas, and much more. This is one of the most important components in Excel, so make sure to practice along with the book and dedicate more time by working on your own before progressing. Take note that even though you might be familiar with mathematical formulas or you're already used to using them in order spreadsheet programs, you should still go through this because there will be a trick or two, even for an expert to learn!

How to Enter a Formula

Formulas are built from five components:

- The operator: Operators are used to write multiplication, addition, subtraction formulas and so on. You can't have a formula without them.
- Cell reference: When you write a formula you use the cells and the ranges in order to refer to the values contained inside them. Take note that you can write a reference to a cell inside your current worksheet, as well as any other worksheet that's either part of the current workbook, or even a different workbook.

- Text or values: In addition to the cell data, you can add your own values as well, or you can add a text string such as "weekly results." Just make sure to add the quotation marks otherwise it won't count as a string and you'll probably get an error.
- Functions: Functions are often used to simplify your work or to write more complex formulas. For instance, you can type SUM, followed by some values inside the parentheses.
- The parentheses: Like in math, they are used to establish an order in which certain operations are calculated.

The first rule you need to remember is that when inserting a formula in a cell, you need to start with an equal sign.

SUM	▾	⋮	✕	✓	ƒx	=SUM(B2:B20)		
◢	A	B	C	D	E	F	G	H
1		Values						
2		2						
3		55						
4		88						
5		55						
6		6						
7		17						
8		8						
9		67						
10		9						
11		345						
12		22						
13		454						
14		676						
15		345						
16		324						
17		54						
18		344						
19		45						
20		675						
21		=SUM(B2:B20)						
22								

This tells Excel that you're about to write your formula. However, the new versions of Excel are a lot more forgiving and even if you don't, the program will attach a leading equal sign once you type the formula. In addition, you can also use the "at" symbol at the start of the formula because that means you're about to use a function. Either way works fine in Excel. Here's an example:

=SUM(B2:B20)

@SUM(B2:B20)

In any case, you'll notice that Excel will actually change the "at" symbol with the equal sign instead. These are just some classic rules that you can still use, because the modern versions will detect them and make the appropriate changes automatically. Furthermore, if you have a cell reference inside your formula, you can add it either manually, or by pointing to it. We are going to explore both methods.

The manual method simply means that you are going to select a cell, add the equal sign, and then write your formula. When you type the formula, everything is displayed inside the cell you're using, as well as Excel's formula bar at the top. Once you finished typing the formula, hit the Enter key to confirm it. The cell you used will now give you the result of that formula. However, when you activate that same cell, you'll see the formula you typed inside the formula bar.

The pointing method refers to typing a formula that holds a number of cell references, so you're still going to introduce some information manually, though not all of it. That's because Excel allows you to "point" to the cell you wish to refer to. Here's how this works if we want to use a simple "=B1+B2" formula:

First you need to move the cell pointer to the B3 cell. Now type the equal sign to start your formula.

If you hit the up arrow, you'll see that Excel moves a border box around the cell. By hitting the up key twice, you'll see the cell reference to B1 and it will appear in the B3 cell, which is the cell where we're typing the formula. Remember, that the formula also appears in the formula bar. And if you don't want to use keys, you can use your mouse to click on the B1 cell to make the reference to it.

Not use the plus sign, then point to the B2 cell, either with your mouse or by using the up arrow. The reference is now added to the formula.

Finally, hit the Enter key to finish the formula. Now you'll see the result inside the B3 cell, where you typed the formula. In order to check up on the formula now, you'll have to look at the formula bar while the cell is selected. You can also cancel your formula by hitting the Esc key on your keyboard or by clicking the X found near the formula bar.

You may think that the pointing method involves too many steps for no reason, but it's actually far more efficient and recommended than using the manual method. You just need to get used to it, but once you do, you'll realize you work faster that way and with fewer errors. After all, accuracy is key when working with data.

Names

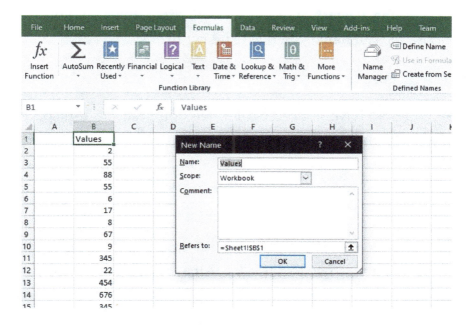

Excel allows us to designate a name to any cell or range we want. This can be handy when writing certain formulas because we can type the name of the cell instead of the reference. To add the name to your formula, you'll just have to move your mouse cursor in the formula where you want it to be placed and use either of these methods:

You can use the Auto-Complete feature when creating your formula. When you have named cells, you can type the first couple of letters and the program will start making suggestions by listing you the options that start with those letters. Take note that default functions like "SUM" are also included in this feature.

The second option involves pressing the F3 key in order to pop up the Paste Name dialog box. From this box you can choose the cell name you need and confirm it.

Using Spaces

As you may have noticed earlier, we don't tend to use spaces when typing a formula. However, it's ok to use them, including line breaks, because they have no impact over the result. It's up to you whether you choose to use spaces. Some people prefer them because it makes the data more readable.

With that being said, if you want to add a line break within the formula you need to use the Alt + Enter keys. There's no need to worry about having too many spaces or line breaks inside a formula because you can actually insert around 8,000 characters without a problem. So, it's highly unlikely that you'll ever pass that limit even if you do use a high number of spaces.

Formula Examples

You can write any formula you can think of using the aforementioned method, as long as you have some basic math knowledge. But just in case we're going to go through a few simple formulas as examples here.

Let's start with a simple multiplication problem like:

=100*.01

The result is 1. Of course, this isn't a very useful example, but you will occasionally perform simple operations, or you might use Excel as a calculator instead of switching to an actual calculator application. We'll talk more about this aspect later.

Next, we have a basic formula that will add the values in three cells and give us their sum:

=A1+B1+B100

Now let's use some named cells:

=Income-Rent

This formula will subtract whatever value is in the Rent cell from the value inside the Income cell.

Next up we can use a function, like the SUM function to add all the values within a range of multiple cells:

=SUM(A1:A25)

Beats typing A1+A2+A3+...A25, doesn't it?

Now let's do something new and use the equal operator to compare the values within the cells. This kind of formula can only give us two results. The comparison can either turn out to be TRUE or FALSE:

=B2=D35

Finally, let's write a slightly more complex formula that changes the order of the operations by using parentheses:

=(A10-A15)*C3

First, we subtract the value from A15 from the value within A10 and afterwards we multiply that result by the value inside the C3 cell.

Think of any other formula you'd like and try it out!

How to Edit a Formula

At some point you'll come across a situation when you need to edit your formulas. This might be due to some modifications you're making to your worksheet, or maybe you're getting some errors that require correcting. Formulas can be easily edited in a similar way you edit cells. Here are a couple of methods:

Simply double-click on the cell containing the formula. This automatically enables you to change the contents of the cell directly. Take note that for this to work you must have the "Double Click Allow Editing Directly in Cells" option to be ticked. It should be by default, but in case nothing happens when you double-click, head over to the Advanced tab inside the Options dialog box and check.

Using the F2 key. Again, this method will allow you to edit the formula inside the cell. Again, make sure the option mentioned above is enabled. If it isn't however, the F2 key will switch you to the formula bar instead, and that's ok as well.

Finally, you can choose the cell you want to edit and then switch to the Formula bar where you can see the formula used in that cell. Remember that cells show results after confirming the formula.

Take note that during the editing process you can select the entire formula or part of it by dragging your mouse cursor or by using your arrow keys while holding the Shift button down. Furthermore, if it's an error you're dealing with and Excel doesn't let you confirm the formula, you need to turn it into plain text and perhaps deal with it later. This might not be ideal, but sometimes it's better to move on with your work instead of being stuck with a faulty formula. So, in order to do that, simply remove the equal sign. You can always add it back when you plan to figure out the problem.

The Formula Bar Can Be a Handy Calculator

As mentioned earlier, if you want to make a certain calculation you don't have to use an actual calculator or open up your favorite calculator application. The formula bar can be used on its own as a calculator. So, for example we are going to type the next formula into any cell we want and then store just the result:

=(110*1.01)/12

As you can see, this formula will return the same result no matter what. So, we can store that result by pressing the F2 key to edit the cell, followed by the F9 key and enter. Now the result is stored instead of the formula. Take note that this method can be applied when working with cell references too, it doesn't have to be solid values.

However, this method is much more useful when dealing with functions instead of just basic formulas.

=SQRT(339)

Here we're trying to determine the square root of 339. Once you input the data in the cell, hit the F9 key, followed by Enter. The result will be recorded on its own. Finally, we can also just take a part of the formula and convert it into a value using the same technique. Write a formula such as the following:

=(222*1.02)/B2

Then select the multiplication operating within the parentheses and hit the F9 key followed by Enter. As a result, the formula will now look like this:

=(226.44)/B2

Formula Operators

The operators are one of the most basic elements used to write formulas and without them we can't really perform any operations. Excel offers support for a number of operators and not just the standard addition, subtraction, division, and multiplication operators we used until now. Here are the rest:

%This is the percent operator that technically isn't an operator under other circumstances. However, in Excel it works like one by dividing any number by a value of 100 if used inside a formula. Otherwise, it's used to represent a percent value.

^This operator represents exponentiation.

& This is translated as text or string concatenation. The operator is used to join strings together. For instance, the concatenation of the strings "Super" and "man" results in the text "Superman."

=The equal sign represents the logical comparison "equal to."

>Another comparison operator that means "greater than."

<This means "less than."

>="Greater than or equal to."

<="Less than or equal to."

<>This strange operator means "not equal to." In other programs the equivalent to this would be !=, but this isn't used in Excel.

While these are typical mathematical operators you may already be familiar with, Excel also offers support for three reference operators:

The colon (:) is a range operator. In other words, it creates a reference to all the cells within a certain range.

The comma (,) represents union. It is used to combine a number of cell or range references to create a single reference.

The single space represents an intersection. In other words, it creates a reference to the cells that are common to two references.

Now let's see some of these operators in action by creating a number of formulas with them.

Let's start with string concatenation in order to create a new string from multiple text strings:

="Figure-"&"42A"

Remember that text strings need to be written in between quotation marks or the formula won't work. In our example we have two strings. The first one is "Figure-" and the second is "42A." By using the & operator we combine them into a single string, namely "Figure-42A." Take note that concatenation also works when used with cell references, not just actual text.

Next up we have the exponentiation operator that is used to raise a value to the specified power and produce a result. Here's a simple example:

=2^3

The result is 8 because we raised the value of 2 to the third power. However, normally you'd use cell data and not direct value calculations. So, you'd raise the value inside certain cells to the specified power.

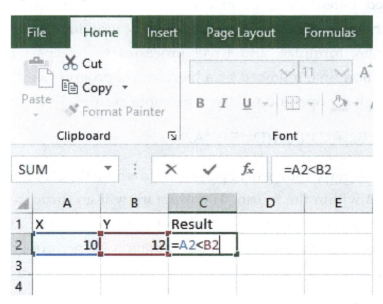

Next, we have the logical operators that can return the value of TRUE or FALSE. Here's a simple example assuming that the value in cell A2 is 10 and the value in cell B2 is 12:

=A2<B2

The result is TRUE because 10 is less than 12. The other logical operators work exactly the same way.

Take note that in Excel we don't have the AND and OR operators. However, you can use functions instead in order to specify them. Here's an example where the result will be true if cell B2 is equal to 10 or 12:

=OR(B2=10,B2=12)

The AND function works the same way.

As a final note on formulas, you need to know how to use nested parentheses, or in other words, parentheses within parentheses. They are needed when working with more complex formulas, and Excel processes the deepest nested operation first, followed by a hierarchical progress as it works through the operations. Here's a simple example:

=((A2*B2)+(C3*D3)+(D4*E4))*A7

Here we have four sets of parentheses where three of them are nested within the fourth. The program will go through every nested set and calculate the sum of the three results. Only at the end will the multiplication operation be performed. You can use nested parentheses as much as you want, even if you don't really need them. We can write certain operations in different ways, but by using nested parentheses we can make the formula a lot easier to read and you're more likely to avoid messing with the order of operations. Here's an example:

=A1*B1+2

As you probably know, multiplications are performed before additions, therefore we don't really need to use any parentheses. However, we should use them anyway because it will look more orderly, and we'll be able to instantly recognize the formula with a mere glance. Here's the difference:

=(A1*B2)+2

Doesn't it look better? It's up to you at end, but most people like breaking their formulas down and organizing them as much as possible.

Excel Charts

We need Excel to store info for small & large businesses as well as personal data. Even though spreadsheets seem to be necessary for data processing, these are cumbersome and do not provide a clear view of data trends & relationships for team members. MS-Excel can assist them in converting spreadsheet details into graphs to create an intuitive research report as well as make rational business decisions.

MS-Excel 2021 helps you to build graphs & charts for almost any purpose. If you've created an MS Excel chart or graph, you could use the Template button to modify and adapt it to your specifications. Learn how to design a map in Excel 2021.

Here are the distinct forms & types of charts?

An Excel graph is a graphical representation of details in bars & several other shapes. It's a visual representation of data from such a workbook which could help you understand the data better than just gazing at the figures. A chart seems to be a powerful tool for visualizing data in a variety of formats, including Bar, Pie, Column, Doughnut shape, Graph, Zone sort, Radar graphs, Scatter dots, & Floor graphs. Using Excel to design a chart is a fast and effective method.

The Pie Charts

In certain cases, pie charts have been used to show the individual significance of different values while still adding the total value. A single collection of data is often used in a Pie chart.

To build a pie chart on some kind of data set using the 2019 or 2021 versions of Excel, simply follow the instructions.

Pick the data set first from the A1:D2 range.

Over the Design tab of the Chart's type, pick the Pie logo.

Click Pie from the menu.

As a consequence, you will note the following.

Press on the pie so as to choose the whole pie. To take a section of the map away from the midline, tap on it.

Note: If you're designing a pie chart with a numeric mark, make sure cell A1 is blank first. While doing so, Excel will not treat the figures within column Too as a dataset &, therefore, will build the correct table automatically. If you like, you can add the content Year during step 1 after you've made the Chart.

Pick the A1:D1 category, then hold CTRL and click the A3:D3 category.

Press Delete on the icon at the bottom of the screen (following the preceding step of adding the graph).

Pick a good pie chart.

Pick a Data labeled check box by clicking the + icon on the desired section of the Chart.

On the appropriate side of the Chart, hit the paintbrush icon to change the color theme of the pie chart.

Right-click, that bar graph, then select Data Label Type from the context menu.

Uncheck value, verify Percentage, then press Middle to evaluate Name of Type.

Column Graphs

To design a column chart within Excel, you'll take the following steps:

Highlight the information you wish to use in the column chart. We picked the range A1:C7 for this case.

There in the toolbar at just the top of each page, select the Insert button. Click a chart from its drop-down menu by pressing the Excel Column chart option within Charts Category. For this case, we went with the very first column chart there in the 2-D Column section (regarded as Clustered Column).

All sales and expense statistics will be reflected in the column chart in the rectangle bar spreadsheet. Vertical blue lines represent sales values, while vertical orange lines represent costs. For certain vertical lines, their values of axes could be seen along the left side of the graph.

Last but not least, let's alter the column chart's explanation.

Click the "Chart Title" link towards the top of a graphic item to adjust the title. One ought to be able to notice that the title can be changed. Put the text you want to appear as the title here. Throughout this example, we will use the term "Sales & Expenses" to build a column chart.

The Line Charts

A bar chart, or a chart containing long bars, is a form of Chart used to visualize the significance of data over time. For example, the accounting team might chart a change in the quantity of cash the company has on hand over time.

First and foremost, ensure that the data is properly formatted before designing a bar chart.

Making use of Smart Draw Add column, pick line graph from the Graph menu.

Select the information file you have to use to generate the Chart, & Smart-Draw will create it for you instantly.

Utilizing Edit Graph tools & double-clicking an imported graph, one could easily alter the legend placement, description and modify the shape of a graph.

Bar Charts

To design a bar graph through MS 2021, you'll take the following steps.

Highlight the information in the cell one would need to use to make a bar chart. We picked a range between A1 to C5 in this case.

Within the toolbar, just at the top of every page, click the Insert button. Select a chart through the drop-down menu by pressing the Excel Bar Chart icon in the Charts group. For this case, we went with the very first bar chart there in the 2-D Column section (regarded as Clustered Bar).

You can also use the bar chart as in horizontal bar spreadsheet, which shows the retail as well as the shelf life of each product. Shelf life is represented by orange horizontal lines, while retail life is represented by blue horizontal lines. Through such horizontal lines, one could notice the axes' values at the bottom of the display.

Eventually, let's update the title of a bar graph.

Hit the "Chart Title" icon near the top of a graphic item to change the title. You ought to be able to recognize that the title can be changed. Put the text you want to appear as the title here. Throughout this example, we'll use the bar graph term as "Product Life."

The Area Charts

The same guidelines apply to Excel graphs & charts. Let's look at an example and see how to design an area chart.

For the area, we possess smart quarterly revenue results.

Choose the details

Go over to the Design category > then to Charts group > Select the Field graph.

Pick Clustered Area Graph through those in the region graph.

Scatter Charts

Choose a selection of worksheets from A1 to B11.

Upon this Insert page, hit the XY chart (Scatter) order logo.

Choose a graph subtype that would not include a graph.

The data within the XY table (Scatter) can be shown in Excel.

Double-check the Chart's data organization.

Check if MS has properly arranged the data by looking at the table.

On a Chart Tools Interface link, press the Turn Column/Row control key if you're unhappy with that of the graph's data entity- the data is backward or flip-flopped. (You can also experiment with the Turn Column/Row feature if you think it would be useful.) It's worth noting that the data is well organized. Increased advertising tends to be linked to increased sales, as seen in the graph.

Annotate the Chart as necessary. Make the Chart more attractive & readable by attaching those tiny blossoms to it. E.g., you might create a chart with a title or a description including the Chart's axes by using the Chart Title & Axes Titles controls. You can add a trend line by tapping the Add Chart Options menu upon a Trendline command icon. Pick the Interface click & then Add Chart Element option to display the menu of Add Chart Element. To access the Template page, one should first select an inserted map item or view a graph sheet.

The Trendline menu would appear in MS-Excel. By pressing on one of several of the accessible trendline options, one can specify the number of trendline and correlation estimates one may need. For e.g., to run any linear regression model, click the Linear button on the keyboard. A Trendline Graph Tools Configuration Tab in Excel 2k7 is where you introduce a trend line. To the scattering plot, add the regression equation.

To monitor how well trendline multiple regressions get measured, just use the ctrl key & text boxes within the Trendline Format panel. Place Intercept = checkbox or textboxes, e.g., may be used to force a trend line to intersect the x-axis after a certain point, such as zero. One could also have Forecast Forward & Primitive texts to emphasize that a trend line can be extended beyond and even before existing data.

Tap on the OK button.

You could barely see the regression details, so it all has been annotated, making it a lot clear.

Bubble Chart

A Bubble graph appears similar to a Scatter graph, but with an additional third column to clarify the scale of the bubbles that depict data points therein data sequence.

The subtypes of the Bubble Chart are as follows:

- Bubbles
- A three-dimensional visual effect bubble
- Stock Chart

Stock style charts, as the name implies, will show price changes in stocks. Nonetheless, the Stocks Chart may be used to show changes in other figures, such as average rainfall or annual temperatures.

Place data into rows or columns in a specific order onto a worksheet to make a Stock graph. To make a simple low high stock chart, for e.g., arrange the data with such as Low-High-Close insert like as Column Names in such an order. The subtypes of the Stocks Chart are as follows:

- High-low-proximity
- Amount of high-low-close
- Volume of Open-High-Close
- Open- closer-Higher-Lower

Surface Chart

When you're trying to figure out which combinations of two variables are the best, a Surface graph will help. Colors & shapes depict regions in the very same way as they do in what seems like a topographic chart.

Follow these measures to build a Surface chart:

Ascertain that almost all divisions, including data series, correspond to integer values. On a worksheet, sort data along rows or columns. The following subtypes are represented on the surface chart:

- 3-D surface area
- Contours
- 3-Dimensional wireframe layer
- Wireframe's contour

Radar Chart

The Radar chart compares the values of several different data series. To generate a radar chart, arrange information in rows or columns upon a worksheet.

The below subtypes are included in the Radar chart:

- Radar & Markers
- Radar Loaded
- Simple Radar

Combo Chart

Such Combo graphs merge two or even more graph formats to generate data easier to understand, especially when there is a lot of it. It's visible from a secondary axis that's easier to read. To make a Combo table, put information in rows & columns upon a worksheet.

The variants of the Combo chart are as follows:

- Custom variations
- Panel Cluster – Line
- Secondary Axis Rows in a Grouped Panel
- Layered Field – Clustered Line

Excel Chart Customization

When the Chart Elements icon (with plus mark symbol) is selected in Excel 2k16-2k21, it presents a list including the main chart things that one can add to their Chart upon on the right-hand side of its built-in screen. To introduce an object to the table, hit the Chart Elements symbol to bring up a list of all Axis through Trendline in alphabetical order.

For e.g., to reconfigure the Chart's title, click on the Follow-up button on the Chart Elements toolbar associated to graph Title to display & choose between the below options upon its Follow-up menu:

Include or reconfigure the chart title just above the plot area, centered above the line.

Just use Focused Overlay Title to add or readjust the chart title at the top of a plot field.

More tools for opening the Format chart. To adjust almost every aspect of title formatting, use the choices that appear when selecting the Rows & Fill, Effects, also Scale & Assets buttons below. Title Choices & Script Layout & Fill, then Text Effects, also Dialog box tabs below Text Options there in the task pane.

The first column of this informational table includes the legend's keys.

How Significant Are the Charts?

MS-Excel has several automated tools, such as a graph function, to cope with all these other data storage values.

Anyone with accessibility to a spreadsheet could change data after it has been processed in the Excel database to view and express its significance. The chart function may be a key component of these systems.

Visualization

Spreadsheet managers may use Excel charts to create visual interpretations of data sets. Users can create various charts upon whom data is graphically depicted by highlighting a collection of data within the Excel spreadsheet & adding it to the graphing feature. Excel charts suitable for management/company presentations would help explain and convey the data set. A chart, rather than a table is containing lines of figures, which provide a clearer view about a set of data variables, allowing administrators to incorporate this interpretation into analysis or even plans.

Customization

MS-Excel simplifies the process of constructing charts from pre-existing data sets. Unless the spreadsheet has already changed data, the chart function might convert it to a graphic with just a minimum amount of user feedback. MS-Suggested Excel's Charts tool is an essential aspect of the phase. With only a few clicks, spreadsheet administrators can generate a chart, pick a chart type, and customize the names & axes.

Integration

When a business or other organization requires a database, data managed within MS Excel may be incorporated using the Excel chart function. For instance, whenever an Excel spreadsheet creates a chart using data in a worksheet, that Chart updates automatically as the data changes. This allows company managers & supervisors to keep track of their data as well as visualizations in a single feature, allowing them to quickly review reports.

Important Things You Can Make in Excel

Outstanding. Long spreadsheets, complex macros, bar graph and the occasional pivot table are likely to come to mind when you hear the term.

Excel has become the technical norm in offices around the world for pretty much everything that needs handling of vast volumes of data, with more than almost one billion Microsoft Office users worldwide.

Think twice if you think Excel is just useful for getting you cross-eyed when staring at a collection of numbers & financial records. Instead of basic spreadsheets, there are a variety of uses for Excel in the industry (and beyond), as Tomasz Tunguz pointed out. In truth, the potential uses seem to be limitless.

We won't be able to compile a collection that includes all of Excel's potential programs (even if you're willing to read a listicle the size of War and Peace).

However, in order to show the strength and flexibility of everyone's favorite spreadsheet tool, we've compiled a list of different ways you should use Excel—both professionally and personally, as well as just for fun.

All About Numbers

For instance, Excel's main function is to work with numbers. Excel allows sorting, retrieving, and analyzing a huge (or even small) volume of data a breeze.

When it comes to using Excel for something numbers-related, there are a few different categories to bear in mind.

- Calculating
- Accounting
- Chart
- Inventory Tracking

Calculating

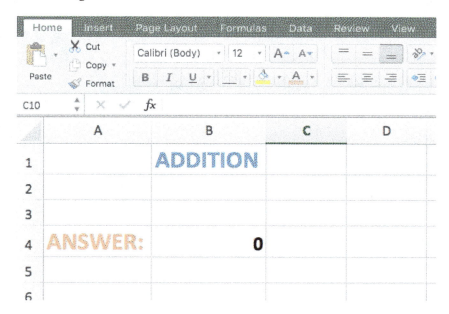

Do you ever find yourself doing the same calculations? By programming your frequently used calculations in Excel, you will build a fully personalized calculator. That way, all you have to do is punch in your numbers, and Excel will calculate the response for you—no effort needed.

Accounting

Budgeting, forecasting, cost monitoring, financial reporting, loan calculators, and other tools are all accessible. Excel was essentially created to satisfy these various accounting requirements. And, given that 89 percent of businesses use Excel for multiple accounting functions, it clearly meets the criteria.

Excel also comes with a variety of spreadsheet models to help you with both of these tasks.

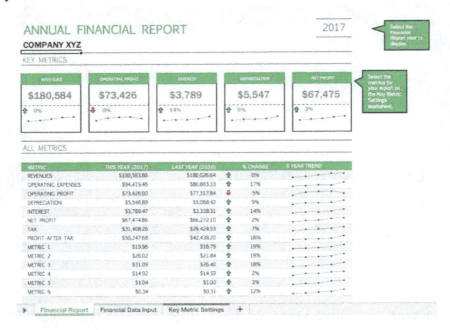

Charts

The number of pie charts, line charts, scatter charts, region charts, bar charts and column charts are endless. Excel's ability to turn rows and columns of digits into stunning charts is sure to become one of your favorite features if you need to represent data in a more visual and easily understandable way.

Want to learn more about the different kinds of charts you can make in Excel? This is an excellent resource.

Budget

% of Income Spent Summary

Total Monthly Income
$3,750
Total Monthly Expenses
$2,058
Total Monthly Savings
$550
Cash Balance
$1,142

55%

Inventory Tracking

Inventory tracking may be a pain. Fortunately, Excel will assist employees, company owners, and even people in staying prepared and on top of their inventory until big problems arise.

Personal Inventory

Name	Insurance Company	Agent Address
[Name]	[Company]	[Address]
Address	Agent	Agent Phone
[Address]	[Name]	[Phone/Fax]
Phone	Company Phone	Agent Email
[Phone]	[Phone]	[Email]
Email	Policy Number	
[Email]	[Policy]	

Item Description	Category	Serial Number	Value
[Item]	[Category]	[Serial #]	[Value]
[Item]	[Category]	[Serial #]	[Value]
[Item]	[Category]	[Serial #]	[Value]
[Item]	[Category]	[Serial #]	[Value]
[Item]	[Category]	[Serial #]	[Value]
[Item]	[Category]	[Serial #]	[Value]
[Item]	[Category]	[Serial #]	[Value]
[Item]	[Category]	[Serial #]	[Value]
Total			$0.00

Making a Plan

Let's get away from the numbers for a moment—Excel will help you schedule and arrange a lot of stuff that doesn't need infinite rows of digits. These are;

- Calendars and Schedules
- Seating Charts
- Goal Planning Worksheet
- Mock-ups

These are explained below;

Calendars and Schedules

If you need to build a content schedule for your blog or website? Are you looking for lesson plans for your school environment? Is there a PTO routine for you and your co-workers? Do you or your family have a regular schedule? Excel can be extremely powerful when it comes to different calendars.

Daily Schedule

Week: [Date]   Start Time: 5:00 AM

	Mon	Tue	Wed	Thu	Fri	Sat	Sun
5:00 AM	Go to gym						
5:30 AM							
6:00 AM							
6:30 AM							
7:00 AM							
7:30 AM							
8:00 AM							
8:30 AM							
9:00 AM							

Seating Charts

Creating a seating chart for everything from a big business luncheon to reception may be a royal pain. Excel, fortunately, will render things a breeze. If you are a real whiz, you will be able to generate your seating chart automatically from your RSVP spreadsheet.

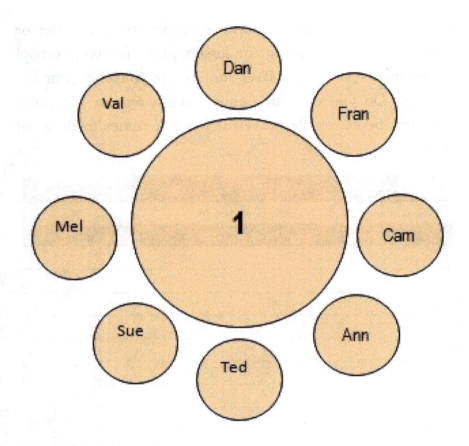

Worksheet for Goal Planning

It helps to have anything to hold you centered and on track, whether it's career goals, health goals, or financial goals. Excel's beauty is revealed. You will use the app to build a variety of worksheets, logs, even planning papers to track your success and, ideally, reach the finish line.

Task	Times/Week	S	M	T	W	T	F	S	Complete
Go for a run	2	✔		✔					Yay!
Don't Leave Dirty Dishes Overnight	2	✔			✔		✔		Yay!
Eat 1 Fruit or Vegetable	3	✔			✔	✔	✔	✔	Yay!
Floss	3	✔		✔			✔	✔	Yay!

8-3-2014

Task	Times/Week	S	M	T	W	T	F	S	Complete
Go for a run	2								0 of 2
Don't Leave Dirty Dishes Overnight	3								0 of 3
Eat 1 Fruit or Vegetable	3								0 of 3
Floss	3								0 of 3

8-10-2014

Task	Times/Week	S	M	T	W	T	F	S	Complete
Go for a run	3								0 of 3
Don't Leave Dirty Dishes Overnight	3								0 of 3
Eat 1 Fruit or Vegetable	4								0 of 4
Floss	4								0 of 4

8-17-2014

Task	Times/Week	S	M	T	W	T	F	S	Complete
Go for a run	3								0 of 3
Don't Leave Dirty Dishes Overnight	3								0 of 3
Eat 1 Fruit or Vegetable	5								0 of 5
Floss	4								0 of 4

Mock-ups

When it comes to programming, Excel may not be the first thing that comes to mind. However, believe it or not, the platform may be used to create different mock-ups and designs. It's a common option for designing website wireframes and dashboards, in reality.

Getting Stuff Done

If you want to increase your productivity? Excel, on the other hand, will come to the rescue with a multitude of functions that can help you manage your activities and to-dos with comfort and organization.

- Task List
- Check List

- Project Management Charts
- Time Logs

Now, we deliberated the above points, which are as given below;

Task List

Say goodbye to the old-fashioned to-do list on paper. With Excel, you can create a much more comprehensive task list—and also track your performance on the bigger tasks you already have on your plate.

MY TASKS	START DATE	DUE DATE	% COMPLETE	DONE	NOTES
[Task]	[Date]	[Date]	0%		
[Task]	[Date]	[Date]	50%		
[Task]	[Date]	[Date]	100%	●	

Checklist

Similarly, you should make a quick checklist to cross off the items you've bought or completed—from a shopping list to a list of to-dos for a future marketing campaign.

PURCHASED?	GROCERIES:
☐	Apples
☐	Tomatoes
☐	Milk
☐	Eggs
☐	Cheese
☐	Bread

Project Management Charts

Excel is a complete beast when it comes to making charts, as we've already said. This principle is often true when it comes to different project management charts.

Excel will help you maintain your project on track in a variety of ways, from waterfall charts to Kanban-style boards (like Trello) to monitor your team's progress.

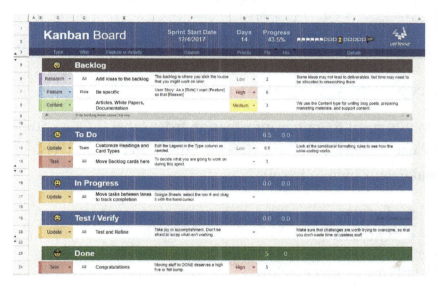

Time Logs

You also realize that keeping track of your time will help you be more productive. Although there are several fancy applications and software to help you fulfill the need, think of Excel as the initial time-tracking application. It continues to be a viable alternative today.

Time Sheet

[Employee name] | [Email] | [Phone]
Manager | [Manager name]

Period [Start date] - [End date]

Standard Work Week	Hours Worked	Regular Hours	Overtime Hours
40.00	0.00	0.00	0.00

Date(s)	▼ Time In	▼ Lunch Start	▼ Lunch End	▼ Time Out	▼ Hours Worked	▼
[Date]	[Time In]	[Lunch Start]	[Lunch End]	[Time Out]	0.00	
[Date]	[Time In]	[Lunch Start]	[Lunch End]	[Time Out]	0.00	
[Date]	[Time In]	[Lunch Start]	[Lunch End]	[Time Out]	0.00	
[Date]	[Time In]	[Lunch Start]	[Lunch End]	[Time Out]	0.00	
[Date]	[Time In]	[Lunch Start]	[Lunch End]	[Time Out]	0.00	

Involving Other People

Do you need to gather information from others? One choice is to use survey tools and forms. Still, don't worry; you will make your own in Excel.

- Forms
- Quizzes

Details are as given below;

Forms

Excel is a wonderful tool for creating forms, from basic to complex. You can also program different drop-down menus so users can choose from a pre-defined collection of options.

Quizzes

Trying to assess someone else's — or even your own — understanding of a subject? You will build a bank of questions & answers in one worksheet and then have Excel quiz you in another.

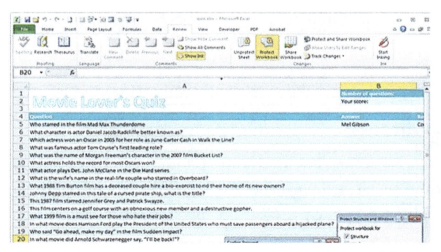

Staying in Touch

Relationship management is vital to your professional and personal growth. Excel, fortunately, makes it easy to stay in contact.

- CRM
- Mailing List

These are explained below

CRM

If you need a simple CRM to keep top - of - mind for your clients? One can be generated in Excel. What's more, the best part? It would be fully flexible if you create it yourself. To support you get started, Sales Hacker has put together a handy series of free sales excel templates.

CRM Template
[Your Name]

Name	Company	Work Function	Phone	Email	Estimated Sale	Last Contact	Next Action	Next Contact	Lead Status	Lead Source	Notes
Jameson, Bill	XYZ Plumbing	Owner	444-555-6666	xyz@plumber.com	$ 45,000	1/10/13		1/29/13	Cold	Referral	
Anderson, Jane	ABC Corp	Sales Manager	222-456-7890	bual@abccorp.com	$ 10,000	1/25/13		2/5/13	Warm	Website	
Smithers, Joe	ACME	Business Dev.	111-234-5678	acme@acme.com	$ 4,500	1/27/13		2/15/13	Active	Email	Loves chocolate

Insert new rows above the gray line

Mailing List

Data does not often have to be numerical. Excel is also excellent at handling and sorting huge lists of names and addresses, making it ideal for the company's holiday party invitation list or the mailing list for a large promotion or campaign.

	FIRST NAME	LAST NAME	ADDRESS	CITY	STATE	ZIP CODE
2	Oprah	Winfrey	123 Magnificent Mile Ave.	Chicago	IL	58922
3	Mister	Rodgers	8935 Beautiful Day Rd.	New York	NY	23935
4	Hulk	Hogan	9284 Hollywood Blvd.	Los Angeles	CA	39825

You may also mail combine using Excel, which allows printing address labels and other resources a lot simpler.

A similar definition may also be used to build folders, RSVP lists, & other rosters that provide a lot of information about individuals.

Just for Fun

It doesn't have to be all work & no play when it comes to Excel. You may make a variety of other interesting items with the spreadsheet tool.

- Historical Logs
- Sudoku Puzzles
- Word Cloud
- Art and animations
- Trip planner

Historical Logs

If you'd like to keep track of the different craft drinks you've tried, the exercises you've done, or anything else entirely, Excel will help you keep it organized and logged.

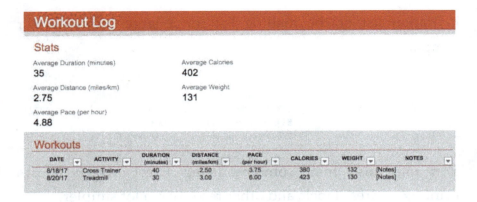

Sudoku puzzles

Do you like Sudoku puzzles? You should make your own in Excel, as it turns out. Alternatively, if you're stuck on an especially difficult one, you may enlist the support of Excel to help you work it out!

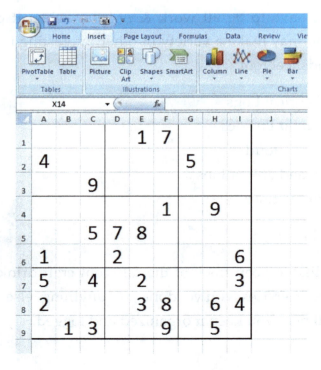

Word cloud

Word clouds aren't the most scientific way to view results. They are, though, an enjoyable (not to mention beautiful) way to learn about the most commonly used words. You guessed it—Excel can be used to create one. Here's how to make a word cloud in Wordle using data from Excel.

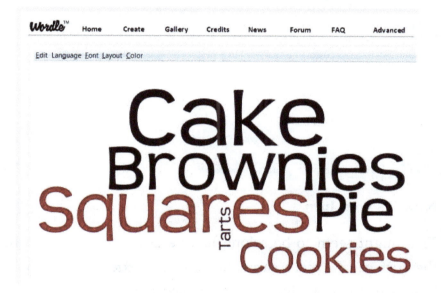

Art and animations

Excel's features are sure to go well beyond what you would expect. Most people have used tools to create some really amazing artwork, ranging from pixelated images to animations.

Trip Planner

Do you have a holiday planned? Before you grab your bags and go, make sure you have it covered by making a handy itinerary. You can also use Excel to create a trip planner framework to ensure you don't forget something (from your budget to airline details).

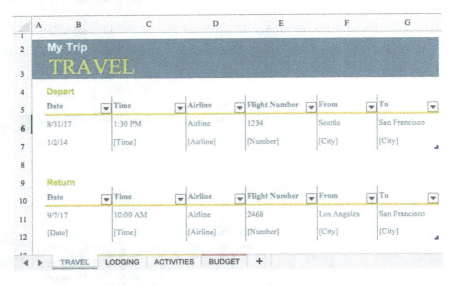

Now it's your turn

This might seem to be a long list. Be assured; it just touches the surface of Excel's capabilities, which extend well beyond basic spreadsheets. Excel may be used for a variety of things, from lists to graphs and charts to concept mock-ups.

Cell Formats and Their Content

L et's look at the Excel screen as we open the program, naming all the elements you see, and making a brief description of them, which will serve as a small glossary of the Excel environment.

Once we have identified the elements with which we are going to interact the most in the use of the program, we will use them to perform one of the most basic, simple and fundamental functions of Excel: to apply formats to a cell or several cells and their contents.

Applying a specific format to the cells is only done to highlight their content over the others, so it does not affect the functionality of the program or its formulas, but helps greatly in the visual aspect, especially if the file ends up being shared with more people who have not participated in its creation.

Finally, we will go on to see some keyboard shortcuts, tricks and combinations of keys that make the user who knows how to use them gain enormously in efficiency.

Excel Environment

Let's look at the image to learn how to recognize and properly name the elements of the Microsoft Excel screen.:

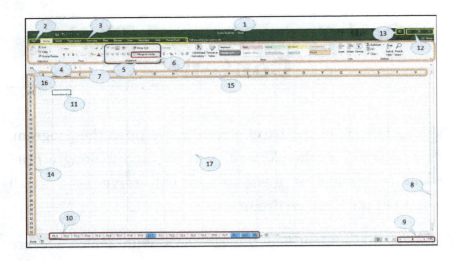

Elements of the screen

1. Title bar: shows the name of the book and sometimes some additional information (e.g., whether the book is networked with other people, whether it is being saved).

2. File tab: is used to access the file information options, open or create files, save, print, etc.

3. Menu tabs: the tabs are sets of commands, i.e., actions that can be performed with Excel, which are grouped logically according to their functionality. Each tab is related to a type of activity.

4. Home tab: is composed of all the groups that are observed, and from here you can perform the most common actions of Excel.

5. "Alignment" group: each tab is made up of different groups, containing commands that act similarly. This group is used to act on the alignment of the cell contents, indentations, height...

6. "Merge & Center" command: the commands are the elements that perform the actions on the selected cells. This command merges the selected cells, going from having several cells to only one, where the content is centered.

7. Formula bar: in Excel you can type either on the selected cell itself or in the formula bar. When the content is a formula, only the result will be shown in the cell, while the formula leading to the result will be shown in the bar.

8. Scroll bar: is used to scroll the sheet up and down (vertical scroll bar), and the bottom scroll bar to scroll left and right (horizontal scroll bar).

9. Zoom: it is used to enlarge or reduce the size of the active sheet on the screen. You can use the bar, buttons or click on the numeric value to enter a value manually.

10. Worksheets: each of the sheets that make up an Excel book. For example, to avoid having to save 12 different books (Excel files) for each month of a year, we can create a single book of the year and create 12 worksheets in that book.

11. Active cell: is the cell we have selected, the one on which the commands we press are applied or the one we write on if we write in the formula bar.

12. Minimize/Restore/Close: as in any program, we have the options to minimize the book, close it or modify the size of the sale (restore).

13. Ribbon Display Options: displays different window display options, such as hiding commands, tabs, both, or showing them back.

14. Rows: each of the 1,048,576 rows that make up an Excel worksheet. They are named with a number from 1 to 1,048,576.

15. Columns: each of the 16,384 columns that make up an Excel worksheet. They are named with a letter starting with A and continuing to Z, after which the column AA, AB, AC... AZ, BA... continues to XFD.

16. Name box: displays the name of the active cell.

17. Cells: an Excel sheet is composed of a multitude of cells, which are the intersections of rows and columns. To name them, first indicate the column (letter) and the row (number) where they intersect.

Manage The Sheets of The Book (Pages)

It is crucial to maintain clarity in our Excel books to know how to properly manage the sheets (or pages) that make up the book. For this it is important to know how to perform all these actions on them:

Renaming the sheets:

This can be done in two ways: either by right-clicking (right-click for right-handed people) on the tab and then clicking on "Rename", or directly by double-clicking on the current sheet name. After this we simply type, press Enter on the keyboard and we have already changed the name of the sheet.

Change the color of the worksheet tab:

Clicking with the right button on the name of the worksheet and then moving the mouse to where it says "Tab Color" displays a palette of colors, where we can choose one of the colors that appear here or click on "More Colors ..." to open an advanced color menu.

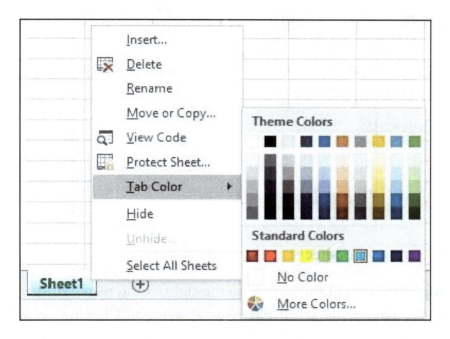

Delete worksheets:

To delete a worksheet, right-click on the sheet you want to delete and then click on "Delete". If the sheet contains any data, a message will appear asking if we are sure we want to delete the sheet, because when we delete a sheet there is no way to recover it (unless we had saved the file with that sheet).

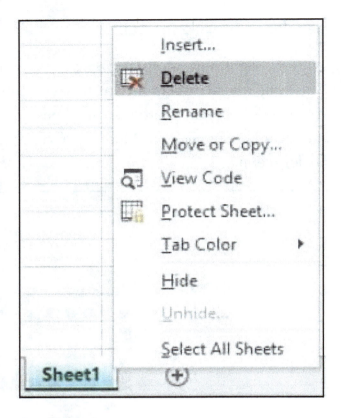

Inserting worksheets:

At the bottom of the screen, to the right of the page labels and to the left of the scroll bar is a "+" symbol. Clicking on this symbol creates a new blank sheet to the right of the selected sheet.

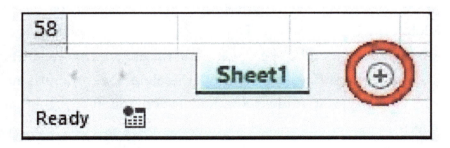

Move/Duplicate worksheets:

If we press with the right button on a sheet and then on "Move or Copy" a new window appears, where we can indicate where we want to move the sheet (the sheet will appear to the left of the sheet we select). If we do this same thing but checking the box at the bottom of the "Create a copy" window, we will add a sheet equal to the one selected where we have indicated.

To make this easier we can simply click with the left button on the name of the sheet and drag (without releasing the left button) to where we want to move the sheet. If we do the same but pressing and keeping the "Ctrl" key on the keyboard, we will duplicate the sheet.

Insert/Delete rows, columns and cells

When we are working with an Excel sheet with a lot of data it is sometimes necessary to introduce new data in the middle of the data we already had introduced. To do this, instead of moving all the preceding data, it is easier to insert a range of blank cells, displacing the preceding cells without deleting them.

This can be done from the "Cells" group on the "Home" tab, where we can insert or delete cells, rows, columns and sheets. To do this it is necessary to select the cell or range of cells where we want to position the new cells and press the button of the desired command.

A quicker way to insert cells or ranges is to select where you want the new cells to be positioned (as before) and press "Ctrl" and "+" simultaneously on the keyboard. To delete, do exactly the same thing but pressing "Ctrl" and "-" simultaneously.

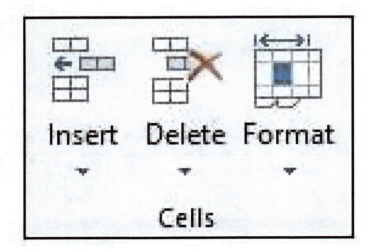

Cell size

By default, all columns in Excel come with a width of 8.43, and rows with a height of 15. In some cases, the size of cells is automatically modified when we perform actions (increasing the size of text in a cell increases the height of the row to fit the height of the text), but we can also change it manually with the "Format" command in the "Cells" group on the "Home" tab. By pressing this command, we can manually enter the height or width of the row or column of the selected cell, as well as "AutoFit" the height or width of the column so that the largest content of the row or column fits right into the row or column without leaving empty space.

Another way to manually enter the width or height is to right click on the letter of the column or row number and select "Column Width..." or "Row Height...". To autofit the size you can also do it faster by double-clicking on the right edge that delimits the width of the column or on the bottom edge that delimits the row number (right image).

Formatting Of Cells

Excel cells are fully customizable in the way they display content (colors, text size, text effects, font...), as well as the alignment of cell content (centered, right, indented...).

The "Font" and "Alignment" groups, both on the "Home" tab, are used to edit the formatting of the cells.

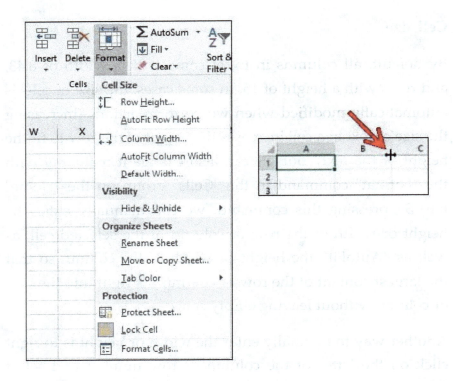

The "Font" group groups the commands to edit cell color, font, size, style (bold, italic...) etc.

The "Alignment" group is used to define the alignment and orientation of the cell contents, and other related commands such as "Merge and Center" and "Wrap Text".

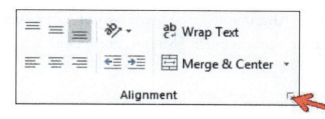

All the font and alignment modification options are accessible from the normal Excel view in the "Home" tab (the groups shown in the prior images). However, if you click on the button in the lower right corner of any of the groups (arrow marked in the earlier image) you can access the cell format menu, from which you can view, by tabs, each of the groups referring to the format of the cells, for a clearer view of what we are modifying thanks to the previewer.

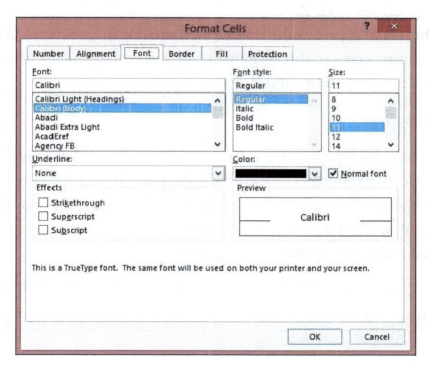

Within the "Alignment" group are two of Excel's most useful visualization commands: "Merge and Center" and "Wrap Text".

Merge and Center:

When several cells are selected, and this button is pressed, all the selected cells are merged and become one larger cell.

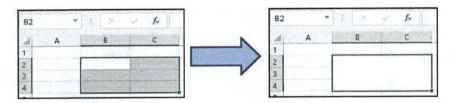

Writing on this combined cell is equivalent to writing on the top left cell (cell B2 in the case of the image), changing only the visual aspect of the sheet, and therefore any reference you want to make to this combined cell should be done as if you referenced the top left cell.

Wrap text:

When you type a text in a cell and it is too long to be shown in the cell two things can happen: if the cells on the right contain nothing the text will be shown "invading" the cells on the right, while if the cells on the right are occupied the text in our cell will be shown only as far as it fits in the cell.

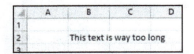 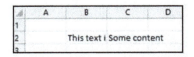

The "Wrap Text" command automatically adjusts the height of the row so that the text fits completely in the cell without changing the width of the column (B2 is wrapped, while C2 is not).

◢	A	B	C	D
1				
2		This text is way too long	Some content	
3				

Manual line breaks in a cell.

In addition to the "Wrap Text" command there is another manual way to type on several lines in a cell. This is done by pressing "Alt" and "Enter" simultaneously on the keyboard when typing in a cell.

◢	A	B	C	D
1				
2		This text is way too long	Some content	
3				

Border Format

Continuing with the customization of the format we arrive at the format of the borders. As we already know, an Excel sheet is made up of a multitude of cells. Each cell is delimited by 4 borders (top, bottom, left and right), which can be marked in different ways or removed completely.

When we create an Excel sheet it appears by default with all the borders marked softly (these borders appear in our Excel sheet, but when printing no border will appear).

If we want to remove the borders to give an image as it will appear when printing what we will do is select the target cells and use the "Fill Color" command from the "Font" group by selecting the white color.

In the "Font" group is the "Borders" command, which is used to apply borders to selected cells. Clicking on the center of the button will apply the last type of border we used to the selected cells. To change the type of border we have to press the downward pointing arrow next to the button, and the options will be displayed as shown in the image:

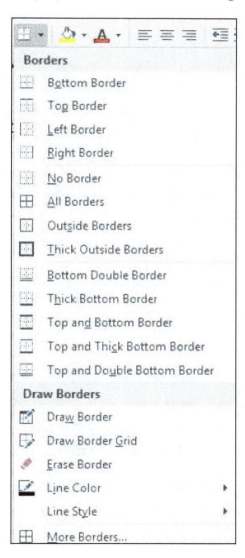

If we click on any of the options under the heading "Borders" the type of border pressed will be applied directly to the selected cells.

At the bottom of the drop-down, under the heading "Draw borders" are these options, useful for drawing "irregular" shaped borders:

Draw border: we can draw borders by hand wherever we want, without having to select the cells first. You can only draw borders in a straight line or in a grid. It is useful to draw borders to several non-consecutive cells without wasting time selecting, choosing the type of border, etc.

Draw border grid: acts in a similar way to the preceding command, with the difference that it also draws the internal lines of the marked grid.

Erase border: clicking on the border of a cell it disappears without affecting the rest of the borders of the same cell.

Line Color: to change the default black color to the border color.

Line style: if we draw borders with the "Draw border" or "Draw border grid" tools these will appear by default with a continuous thin line. If we want to change the line style, we have to select the line style we want from this option.

More borders: from here we can see all the borders of the selected cells and edit them in the most precise and faster way. When we click on it the following menu appears in a new window:

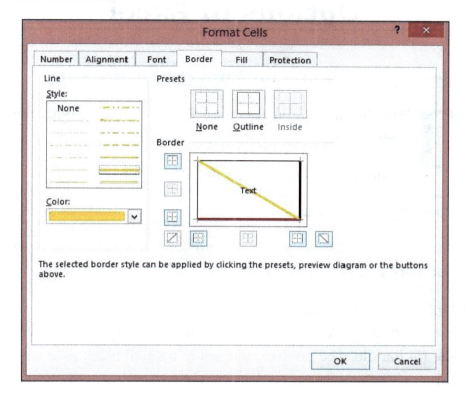

Following the order of the screen, we select the style of the border (normal, discontinuous, thick, double...), the color and we keep on clicking in the window where it puts "Text" drawing ourselves the border with each click.

Advanced Formatting Options in Excel

Use of Fill Handle for Copying Formatting

The filling handle functions in combination with the mouse. Filling the handle uses include:

Copying and formatting details

Copying of formulas

Fill the cells with a variety of numbers, like odd and even numbers, and several more.

Highlight the cell(s) containing the data to be copied or extended in the case of a series. Place the mouse pointer over the fill handle. The pointer changes to a small black plus sign (+).

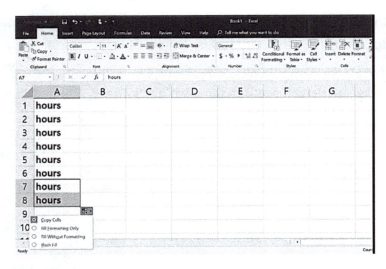

Highlight that cell(s) holding that data to be copied and expanded in that case of a sequence.

Place a mouse pointer over that filling handle. The pointer switches to a tiny black plus (+) symbol.

Click and holding down that left mouse button icon; drag the fill handle to the desired cell (s).

Use of Paste Option for Copying Formatting

Another easy way to copy that format to MS-Excel is to use the keyboard shortcuts for the Paste Special > Formats:

Pick the cells from which you like the format to be copied.

To copy that chosen cells to the clipboard, click Ctrl + C.

Pick the cell(s) where the format must be used.

Tap Shift + F10, S, R in MS-Excel 2010-2019, and then tap Enter.

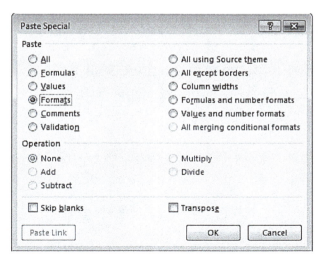

Copying Style Between the Workbook

Creating the MS-Excel format style would save a lot of time, particularly if you would have various custom formatting specifications. You may assume that you need to re-create these types for each workbook, but you do not. If you would establish that style, you could copy it to another workbook— you do not have to go through the hassle of re-creating that style into the workbook files. Here's how to clone the style:

Open all workbooks—a source workbook that incorporates the pattern and the target workbook you intend to copy a style.

Choose Design from the Shape menu in a Destination Workbook.

Only press Combine.

Choose a workbook that includes that current style(s) you wish to duplicate in a corresponding Merge Style dialog box.

Double click OK.

Look on the home page icon, press Cell Style in that Styles Group. Merge Style is situated at the bottom of the resultant pane.

At this stage, a destination workbook includes all of the custom styles of that source workbook and then starts formatting!

Create Your Custom Format for Data That Is Readable

Let suppose you may have codes that consist of five digits. Instead of form 00041, only type 41 and then let MS-Excel adding the leading zeros.

Join a value of 41 in cell A1.

Pick cell A1, right-click, then tap Cell Format.

Choose Tradition.

Type in the following numbers format code: 00000

Select the OK tab

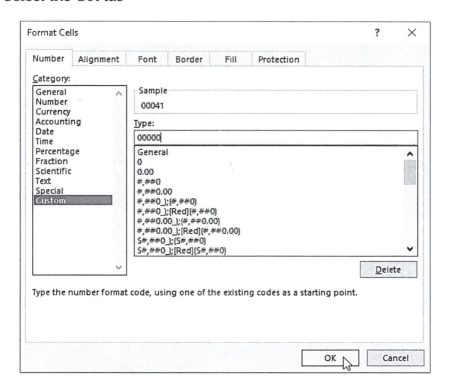

A1		:	×	✓	f_x	41			
	A	B	C	D	E	F	G	H	I
1	00041								
2									

Creating Cell Style Indicating a Purpose

You may also add the theme to the cell or the sequence of the cells. There are many defaults cell types in MS-Excel.

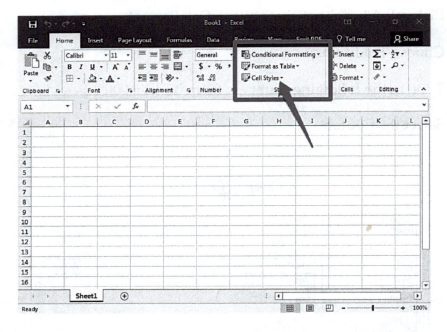

To add a basic cell style:

Pick the cell(s) you want to format.

Tap on the required cell styles. That Two cells would have the styles added in that screenshot below.

"Good" cell means that data in that cell is either good or correct.

The "Check" cell means you will need to validate the detail in that cell.

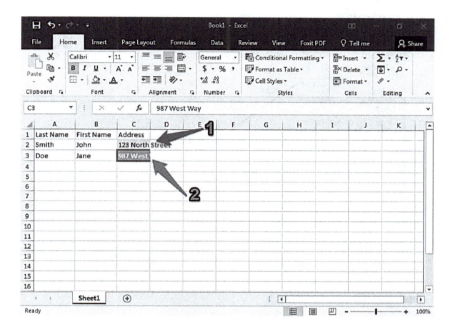

Verifying Page Orientation

In excel, Page orientation applies to how the production of the page is written. If you alter that orientation, it will immediately switch to the current paper orientation on page breaks. To check the orientation of that page:

Go to the Style tab of the website and then to the orientation portion.

When you tap on the orientation tab, you can see the drop-down of two portrait and landscape choices, which are already selected and highlighted.

See the illustration below where the image is already picked, which implies that the direction of your existing document is now a portrait.

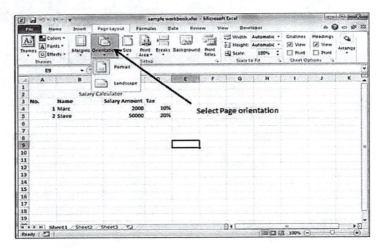

Putting Page Break

To access the boundary and region control mode, you have to go to that "VIEW" tab and pick that "Page Break Preview" method in the Workbook Views portion.

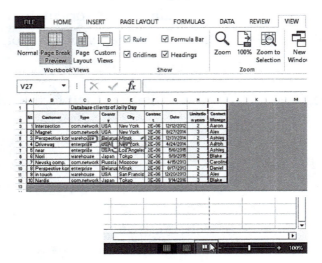

The second choice is to press on the third switch on the MS-Excel pane status bar's right side.

You have to set and correct page layout borders that will divide all areas to identify a print area. In doing this, press the blue dotted lines into the Page Break Preview display and shift it to the appropriate location, holding down a left mouse button Icon.

	F	G	H	I	J
'			←╫╪→		
	Contrac t	Date	Limitatio n years	Contact Manage	
·k	2E+06	12/12/2012	2	Aaron	
·k	2E+06	8/27/2014	3	Alex	
◢	2E+06	12/31/2014	2	Ashley	
·k	2E+06	4/24/2014	5	Aaron	

If a table reaches past the white field, anything in the gray area would not have written. If you are in the Page Split Preview display and all that data is in the gray field, you can get a blank paper while printing. You may delete a print region manually by dragging this boundary between both the gray and white areas.

Define the print field, set the boundary, and change it. How do I apply boundaries (page breaks)? Press on a cell where the database break must be placed and select the alternative "Insert Page Break."

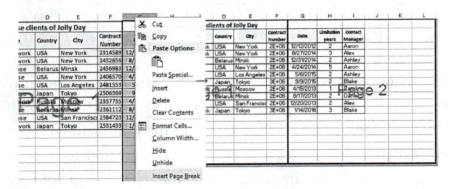

In what way can we incorporate the vertical page break? Right-click on a column where a border is to be placed, select the identical option: "Insert Page-Break." To insert the horizontal page split, you can do the same thing—click on a header of a certain row.

Note. A "Reset Print Area" choice is available in a context menu. It enables you to remove all text breaks and change the default settings. Use this to start over again.

How to View the Preview Option

Choose the File page. The backstage view will be shown

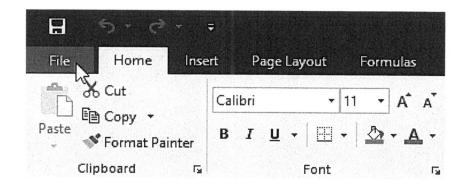

Choose Print. The Print panel will be shown.

And you'll see your preview just on the right side of a window that can be changed according to your needs.

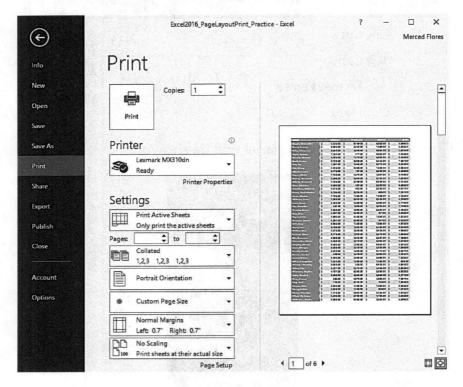

You may use the following to arrange a printing area. The latest page orientation would be shown in the Overview panel.

Navigate to a Print panel. In our case, we can observe in the Preview panel that our material will cut off when it is printed.

From the Page Orientation drop-down panel, choose the appropriate orientation. In our Instance, we're going to choose Landscape Orientation.

Settings

Print Selection
Only print the current selecti... ▾

Pages: [▲▼] to [▲▼]

Collated
1,2,3   1,2,3   1,2,3   ▾

Portrait Orientation ▾

Portrait Orientation
Landscape Orientation

No Scaling
100 Print sheets at their actual size ▾

Page Setup

The updated page orientation will now be shown in the Overview panel.

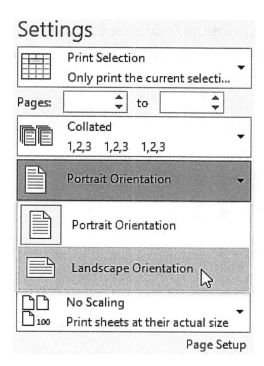

Simply Navigate for the Print panel. In our case, we can easily see in our Preview panel that our whole content is shown as cut off when it is printed.

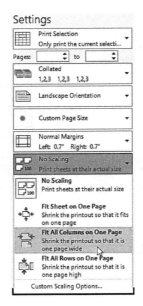

Make a selection of your own choice from the dropdown menu used for Scaling. In our example, we have selected the Fit All Columns option from the drop-down list.

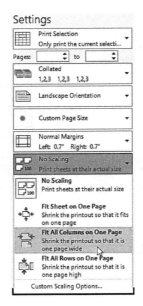

The workbook will be simplified to fit onto the single tab.

Set or Clear the Print Area for Your Spreadsheet

To Set the Area

Pick the number of cells you'd like to set as a print region in the MS-Excel worksheet.

Go to Web Configuration -> Web Setup -> Display Region -> Print Area Setup.

It will set all the selected cells to the print region and will create a named set for the chosen region as well.

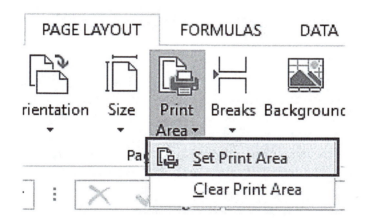

To Clear the Area

Select somewhere on the worksheet where you'd like to clear the printing regions.

Go to Web Configuration –> Web Setup –> Print Field –> Print Area.

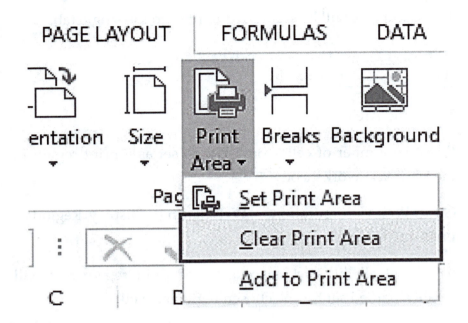

Moving Your Worksheet Within the Same Workbook

If you always have moved the sheet from one workbook to another, you might have used a right-click menu Icon to pick Transfer or Duplicate. But you will simply drag and drop a sheet directly to some other spot within or outside of the workbook.

Only click on a tab that has the name of a sheet on it.

Next, hold a mouse button icon down as you drag that mouseover.

And then drop it anywhere you wish it to be in the latest workbook.

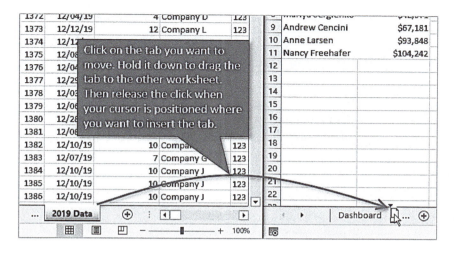

This method transfers the sheet entirely and does not leave a duplicate copy in the "from" workbook. Although, if you wish to leave a sheet and create a duplicate of it on a new sheet, the procedure is just as simple.

Copying Your Worksheet Within Your Workbook

If you want to copy a certain Worksheet, copying all that Worksheet contents to the current Worksheet follows the measures below.

Right-click a Worksheet tab you would like to copy at the bottom of the MS-Excel pane.

Select the move button or Icon for Copy.

In a Move or Copy pane, pick that Worksheet where you'd like to put the copied Worksheet in the before sheet column.

Check a Create Copy choice window, then press OK

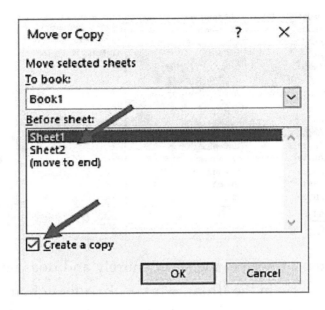

A worksheet duplicate is inserted and positioned before a Worksheet that you choose in step three above. E.g., if you have two worksheets known as "Sheet1" and "Sheet2," you choose Sheet2 in Process 3, other copies of Sheet2 will be put in place of Sheet1. The outcome will look like an image of the illustration below. That "Sheet2 (2)" Workbook is the clone of Sheet2.

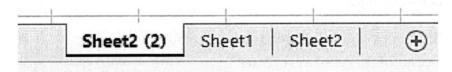

Pivot Table

Before starting I want you to know that Pivot Tables are not a "beginner thing". Instead, you need to really become more familiarized and comfortable with all the topics inside this book before attempting to become a Pivot Table superstar.

Here you are going to learn to create powerful Pivot Tables out of a big database, and it is going to save you lots of wasted time, and, as you may know, time is money! So, you are going to end up saving money and gaining powerful insight on the data you have.

What Is Exactly a Pivot Table?

A Pivot Table is a DYNAMIC TABLE that is shaped according to your needs. In other words, you create a Pivot Table with some clicks and dragging some items, and you get to visualize the information you want, in the shape you want, ordered as you want in a matter of seconds.

The main fact here is that those "clicks and dragged items" MUST BE THE CORRECT ONES! If you screw it up and do it incorrectly, you will get a huge mess.

Where Does a Pivot Table Come From?

You have to know that a Pivot Table is created out of a DATABASE. In other words, THE DATABASE FEEDS THE PIVOT TABLE, always remember that.

As an example, here you have the database that we're going to be using during this (obviously it is going to have more rows). Notice that is has 5 columns or categories, if you will: Name, Quarter Paid, Studio Company, Salary and Bonus.

NAME	QUARTER PAID	STUDIO COMPANY	SALARY	BONUS
CHRIS EVANS	Q1	Lions Gate	97392	5254
ROBERT DOWNEY JR	Q2	20th Century Fox	89754	5329
JENNIFER LAWRENCE	Q3	Universal Studios	78008	7092
CHANNING TATUM	Q4	Metro-Goldwyn-Mayer	98783	5437

GEORGE CLOONEY	Q3	Paramount Pictures	79821	5354
JOHNNY DEPP	Q4	Warner Bros	78171	7345

Just imagine that you are trying to solve these questions, WITHOUT Piot Tables, just using the Filters:

- How much bonus was paid each Quarter?
- How much bonus was paid by each Company?
- How much was paid in Salaries in the third Quarter by Lions Gate company?

Well, you would have to take some minutes to sort, filter and perform each calculation in order to get all those answers, but using Pivot Tables you could have all the answers in less than 1 minute! (Once you have already mastered Pivot Tables, of course)

In order to answer the 1st Question "How much bonus was paid each Quarter?" your Pivot Table would look like this:

Row Labels	Sum of BONUS
Q1	43284
Q2	92146

Q3	67624
Q4	69233
Grand Total	272287

Notice how I created a simple nice Pivot Table, which took 20 seconds of my time to build, and I got the answer, without mistakes.

That is the awesome power a Pivot Tables!

How To Create a Pivot Table?

That is exactly what we are going to do now. Earlier to start creating it, these are the requirements:

A Database with all the data. Remember that the Database feeds the Pivot Table.

The questions you are trying to answer: Begin with the end in mind, to do that you need to be aware of what you are trying to discover. For the exercises, we are going to answer the 2 questions:

- How much bonus was paid by each Company?
- How much was paid in Salaries in the third Quarter by Lions Gate company?

Creating a Database Using an Excel Spreadsheet

How Relational Database Functions

The hierarchical framework of MS-Excel lends itself very well to how the databases function. The database is a list of linked objects (spreadsheet) that, once associated, generates a particular document (row) inside a set of multiple records (table). Each spreadsheet, on its own, is the database, but not a hierarchical one. To sum up, in simple words, we can say that a relational database is the mixture of a Master spreadsheet table and its subordinate tables, including word documents.

Relational Database and Its Applications

Relational databases are designed to understand the association between already stored knowledge objects in data. This allows you to easily retrieve and scan for relevant details, display the same data collection in several forms, and minimize data errors and redundancy.

There have been a variety of explanations for building relational databases. Its most noticeable features are that you don't duplicate the same details on your workbook spreadsheet. E.g., it is repetitive, extremely time taking to copy and paste every driver's name and birth date from a Master database to several Slave databases. But even though you copy the details from one to the next, it also consumes unnecessary storage space and memory, slowing it down. Often, a name and date of birth are not special. For example, hundreds of Jacks Scott, John Smiths, or any of them may easily share their same birthplace. You're only using a license plate. You can't distinguish the drivers. Then you're required (to be secure) to use almost all three fields

Our key purpose for relational databases should be to build queries and indexes that really can retrieve and print unique details. Maybe your supervisor needs a survey that reveals someone in Santa Rosa City, Florida, with traffic violations above $300, or even how many Pensacola riders had new license dates in December? Without a relational database ability, you'd have had to copy and paste the details together through three or more-word documents to that fourth spreadsheet and keep hoping you're all done, and your supervisor doesn't claim, "We say Sarasota County, never Santa Rosa County."

A Simple Example of the Database

A database is normally known as the data stored in a spreadsheet in rows and columns for fast browsing, sorting, and editing. But how can you render a database in MS-Excel?

Any material in a report is stored in the following field and records:

Record is the database (DB) line that contains details regarding a specific entity.

The field is Indeed the column in the database holding the same sort of knowledge for all items.

Records and archive areas are both the lines and the columns of the regular MS- Excel spreadsheet.

				Sales report					
			Managers	January	February	March	April	May	June
		1	Aaron	20450	27298	23501	27966	23709	18789
		2	Alex	0	0	8445	10050	12230	10583
Records DB		3	Ashley	14017	13223	16876	20082	20189	15299
		4	Blake	30892	28993	34557	41123	35234	29808
		5	Caroline	27738	26775	29901	35582	32830	25405
		6	Daniel	15606	14255	17118	20370	16955	15341
		1		2	3	4	5	6	7

Columns DB

In this database records 6 and 7 columns

What Is Meant by a Master Database?

To remind you about how well that MS-Excel database functions, we'll explore two tables—a master table and an information table. The main table is the one that usually includes critical data. This table scarcely updates unless, say, to introduce or remove entities.

With any record in a master table, several records in the information tables (also known as slave or infant tables) connect all to the master table. It's considered a one-to-many friendship. The data throughout the comprehensive tables— such as regular revenue, product values, or quantity—often fluctuate continuously.

To stop repeating all of the master details in each detail chart, build a partnership using a single area, including the Sales ID, and then let MS-Excel do the rest. For, e.g., you have ten sales staff who all have specific demographic details (main table). Any sales individual has 200 items that the employee is selling (detailed and child table). Only at the end of every year, you need the report detailing the overall annual sales by the individual, but you'll need that report outlining the overall sales by region.

Creating a Database in Excel Along with the Use of Filters

The figure below displays two sheets of relevant details. As you'll see, any record in Regular Totals includes a meaning that is further explained by date, staff, and city. Site documents show the cities from each country. Today, assume you would like to total those values by area for Everyday Totals.

Working with the information won't always be that easy. I have intentionally kept this example straightforward to maintain concentration mostly on steps.

	A	B	C	D
1	Date	Value	Personnel	City
2	1/31/2012	$1,480	James	Rochester
3	2/29/2012	$1,908	Luke	Charlotte
4	3/31/2012	$1,582	Martha	Seattle
5	4/30/2012	$1,979	James	St. Louis
6	5/31/2012	$1,440	Luke	Dallas
7	6/30/2012	$1,926	Martha	Boston
8	7/31/2012	$1,833	James	Tampa
9	8/31/2012	$1,190	Luke	Cleveland
10	9/30/2012	$1,128	Martha	Louisville
11				
12				

	A	B	C	D	E
1	Region	City			
2	Northeast	Portland			
3	Northeast	Rochester			
4	Southeast	Chattanooga			
5	Southeast	Charlotte			
6	Southeast	Tampa			
7	Southwest	Dallas			
8	Southwest	Sacramento			
9	Central	Des Moise			
10	Central	Louisville			
11	Central	St. Louis			
12	Northwest	Seattle			
13	Northwest	Billings			
14					

Converting Data to the Tables

Tap somewhere in the data range and tap the Insert button.

Tap on the table in the group of tables.

Tap quite well in that resulting dialog box displayed in the figure below. That header choice is already tested in this situation. When implementing that technique to your very own results, you may also want to test or uncheck this choice properly.

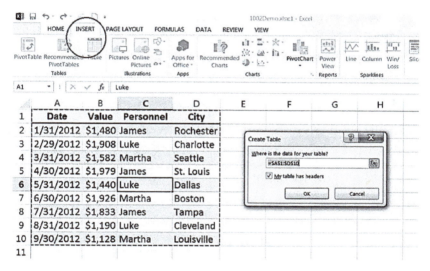

Tap inside that table and tap the Interface background key. Then type the meaningful name in that named area of the table, as seen in that figure below. Call that Daily Totals Table as well as that Sites Table.

There are no geographic details in the data collection that includes the values you would like to outline. This isn't an issue with data modeling. What you need now is a connection between the tables and the values you want to analyze and the geographical information you can use to analyze such principles.

Creating the Relations

First of all, press the Data tab.

Even in the Data Tools category, tap Relationships. (If this alternative is dimmed, go back to #2 and build a table.)

Select Daily Total Table from that first table dropdown.

Select "City" into that Column (Foreign) dropdown.

Select "Site Table" in that Linked Table drop-down.

Select "City" as seen in Figure D in that Linked Columns (Primary) drop-down.

Select the OK tab.

Select close to move back to that sheet.

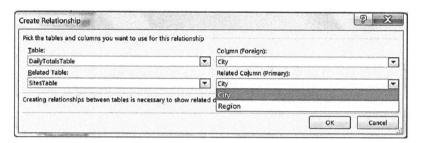

Specify each column that perhaps the columns share to create a relationship inside those two tables.

We can create another Pivot Table to describe the values. Tap the Total Daily Table in and select the Insert key. Select Pivot Table throughout the Tables group, as MS-Excel presents the dialog seen in Figure E, press OK.

At this stage, the pivot Tables framework presently tests one more table, Daily Total Tables. Add Site Table to the following:

Tap the connection and MORE TABLES.

Press Enter in that resulting dialog. Doing so requires a modern data modeling functionality.

As you'll see in the following image, both tables also are part of the layout of the pivot table.

PivotTable Fields ▼ ✕

Choose fields to add to report:

⚙ ▼

☐ Date
☐ Value
☐ Personnel
☐ City

MORE TABLES...

Drag fields between areas below:

▼ FILTERS	‖‖ COLUMNS
≡ ROWS	Σ VALUES

☐ Defer Layout Upda...   UPDATE

Now information models function will be enabled by clicking on Further TABLES

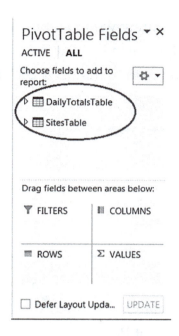

Adding the Fields

It is indeed time to start incorporating the Pivot Table areas. Next, press the Extend arrow to that left of the Daily Total Table to access its fields. Check for Importance and City. Using the scroll bar to navigate the Site Table.

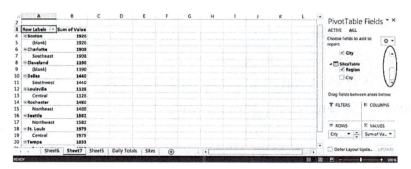

That data modeling function helps you to connect features from both the table to that Pivot Table frame.

That Pivot Table definitely won't be flawless at this stage, but it's time to begin adjusting a bit. The figure indicates the effect of pulling that region field to that COLUMNS segment.

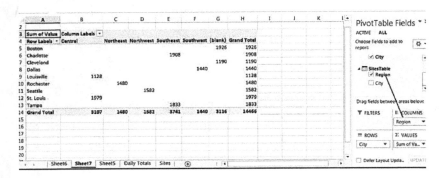

If you don't like this style, you can easily swap column and line headers. Drag that City field to that COLUMNS portion and the Area field to that ROWS section, as seen in the figure.

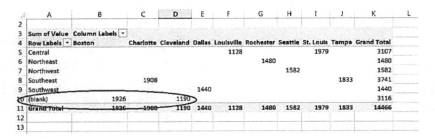

When you pay careful attention, you may have seen the (blank) lines. Can you guess and tell where these lines are originated? One can easily diagnose a problem arising by the question or analyzing those community headers for certain products. Use the figure given below. You will decide that there is no area of importance for Boston but Cleveland.

Luckily, this is a quick fix. See below, adding the values to a Table.

	A	B	C
1	**Region** ▾	**City** ▾	
2	Northeast	Portland	
3	Northeast	Rochester	
4	Southeast	Chattanooga	
5	Southeast	Charlotte	
6	Southeast	Tampa	
7	Southwest	Dallas	
8	Southwest	Sacramento	
9	Central	Des Moise	
10	Central	Louisville	
11	Central	St. Louis	
12	Northwest	Seattle	
13	Northwest	Billings	
14	Northeast	Boston	
15	Central	Cleveland	
16			

1.) Position the cursor in the last column of the last row.
2.) Press Tab to automatically enter a new record into the table.

Reload that Pivot Table after introducing new regional documents. To do so, tap inside that table and then tap the Analyze context menu. In that Data Group, tap the Refresh button.

Filters Options

From this step, you can even filter the required cities by tapping on a filter option with an arrow at the top row with the name "city" and selecting that desired city with filters. If you wouldn't want to use the filters and see all that results, start deleting your selection and choose the "select all" choice.

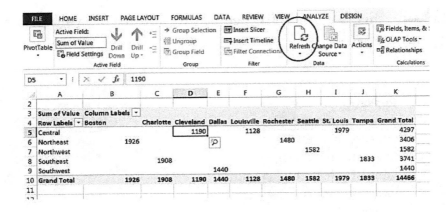

Sum of Value	Column Labels									
Row Labels	Boston	Charlotte	Cleveland	Dallas	Louisville	Rochester	Seattle	St. Louis	Tampa	Grand Total
Central			1190		1128			1979		4297
Northeast	1926					1480				3406
Northwest							1582			1582
Southeast		1908							1833	3741
Southwest				1440						1440
Grand Total	1926	1908	1190	1440	1128	1480	1582	1979	1833	14466

By refreshing your pivot, the regional values would be shown correctly.

Do you see that little magnifying glass symbol in that figure above? Pressing that will help you drill further into the information which is not currently available. Tapping this icon with that value of the chosen Cleveland will show the dialog.

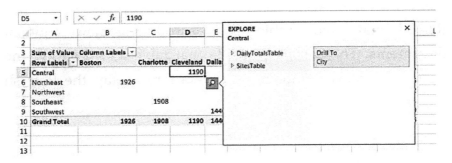

That dialog is set to the Sites Table by default; however, you may switch to Daily Total Table.

Sum of Value	Column Labels			
Row Labels	Cleveland	Louisville	St. Louis	Grand Total
Cleveland	1190			1190
Louisville		1128		1128
St. Louis			1979	1979
Grand Total	1190	1128	1979	4297

Input Masks Being Employed for Data Entry

Input Masks

The input mask seems to be a type of variable that depicts the correct format of the input values. In table areas, query fields, and sort or report controls, input masks may be used. As almost an entity resource, the entry mask is held.

There are three fragments to the input mask.

Each part of the input mask is separated by a semicolon, with one mandatory component & two optional sections. The following is the target of each section:

The very first aspect of this is needed. It includes placeholders and basic information, including certain brackets, intervals, & hyphens, as well as mask icons or strings (a series of characters).

Section two remains optional & pertains to the embedded mask characters & how they were saved in the area. If a second component has been set to 0, the characters become saved along with the data, while if it is set for 1, the symbols will be only displayed and just not saved. Setting the second part to 1 would reduce the server's storage space.

The third element of the input mask remains optional, and it depicts a particular entity or space to use as a buffer. By default, Access uses the underscore (_) character. If you're using a different character, place it in the third section of your masks.

Let's pretend it's a phone

Number input mask in a US format (999) 000__000;0; -:

There are two placeholder elements in that Mask: 9 & 0. Each 0 denotes a necessary digit, while 9 denotes an available digit (that further makes it easier to enter an area code).

The 0 within the second aspect of the input masks denotes that mask characters were mostly saved with the data.

• The third part of the input mask specifies that the (-) hyphen might be used in place of the underscore (_) as the substitute characters.

Input masks are characterized by the characters

The following info explains the placeholder as well as the basic characters for input masks and how to keep track of data entry.

0: The client must insert a bit from the range (0 to 9).

9: A digit from the user must be inserted (0 to 9).

#: The consumer may type an integer, space, or a plus / minus sign. If the application is not received, space will be avoided.

L: The customer is supposed to write a message. You have the choice of typing a letter.

C: The user has Access to characters or holes.

;-/: Thousands of placeholders, date/time separators, & decimal. In MS Windows, the character you are using is dependent on certain sets.

<: All characters that have been followed by that of the upper case are included.

<: Lowercases of just about all the characters that come after it. This makes it possible to fill the input mask from left to right instead than through left to correct.

\: Impeccably matching certain characters that are seen.

": Characters enclosed in double quotation marks would be shown as they are.

Where Possible, Avoid Using Input Masks

Input masks, as useful as they are, aren't always appropriate. You cannot utilize an input mask if any of the following requirements apply to anyone:

An input mask doesn't quite make exceptions while users have to insert data that would not match the Mask.

Some Date Picker controller including a Date or Time area is on your to-do list. A Date Picker controller does not accept input masks.

By Using Mask Wizard, Generate an Input Mask

In Microsoft Access 2k16, like future versions, such as 2k19 or 2k21, you'll just use the so-called Input Mask to create input masks. The input mask has been a set of basic guidelines which determines what type of data would just be submitted in a given field.

Any input mask of (999) 000--0000, for instance, maybe needed to determine how telephone numbers get inserted. The area code is required in this case; however, its numbers must also be entered. This is because a 9 denotes an obligatory number, while a 0 denotes a necessary number in any input mask.

In the Albums chart, we could now introduce an embedding sheet to the Release Date area. The input mask will confirm that users entered every other album's official Date in the appropriate format.

Consider Turning on the design chart

To do so, tapping that Release Date area as shown in the picture. The properties for this region are shown in the bottom picture.

Within bottom frame, hit the Input Masks lines. A mini-icon containing three dots would appear. Using the wizard, the Input Mask Wizard is enabled.

Select the [...] tab having three dots.

This same Input Wizard Mask gives you many options on how the data should be processed. One could choose any choice and test it at the bottom of the wizard in the Try Its section.

Pick the Medium Date & afterward click Next.

The next screen enables you to alter the input mask. You could test any configurations in the wizard's Try Its section at the bottom.

We're going to make one minor adjustment.

To make the input mask, link two zeros: 99->L<LLL-0000

This depicts that the consumer entered that Date using 20-Mar-2016 (DD-MMM-YYYY for e.g.

Once you're happy with the feedback mask, tap Next.

An Input Mask Wizard should show you the most recent view.

Alternatively, hit Finish or End.

When the Input Mask Wizard has been closed, you would see the newly created Interface Masks in the Project Folder with the Input Masks property.

Introducing Input Mask, A Question or Statement

For query

Within your navigation window, right-click the data you choose to change & choose the Design display from the menu bar.

Carry the cursor throughout the column for the database interface grid area you want to turn to. You can even have the cursor go through each row within this field.

F4 will take you to the property document for that area.

Upon this General tab of the Field Properties set hit a Feedback Mask properties key.

To open the Input Mask Wizard, push the Create key. Also, pay careful attention to the instructions in the information already given.

For Reporting

Right-click the type or report you to intend to alter within Navigation Pane & choose template view from the shortcut menu.

Right-click a Control you want to modify and select Properties. Then, on a shortcut menu bar, pick the Properties option.

Click on the Input Mask property button over an All tab.

Hit the Build icon to launch an input mask wizard, cautiously observing the wizard's instructions.

Customizing An Input Mask

First, create a new form or change an existing one to have the custom input mask.

The input masks could only be used on the single line's text field.

Now, for just a single line, drag & drop the text.

After that, pick the form area to enter its Field Options box by dragging it.

Pick the field choice now for forwarding. The Input Mask choices are found within the Advanced field tab.

At this stage, you must mask the Input.

E.g., if you need an eight-digit number, you could enter eight 9s there in the Input Mask field.

So, when the form becomes available on the web, users can see an underscore mark next to each relevant digit.

We've used the number "9" within this example, so only numbers are permitted.

Using Certain Field Property Configurations to Customize Input Masks

A column has been the name for a field within a table. It is a constant characteristic for the records within a table. An average of 225 fields can be added to just a single table by a user. Each field added to the table has a number of options that give you more control over the outcomes. A guide here about how to establish the field within a table can be found here:

Pick "View" from the Home ribbon, then "Design View. "You'll now be asked to change the table's title. Put the title here.

The properties box displays at the bottom section of a table design view when you choose a field.

Use the Field Layout feature to change how your data is displayed on the screen and when it is recorded.

Illustrations Of Input Masks

Consider the following scenario: Many people are unaware that zip codes in the United States include a four-digit suffix. As a result, we do not want it. As a result, we'll use the "9" character to indicate that this data is optional.

Utilizing An Email Address-Specific Input Mask

Pick "View" through the Ribbon section and then "Design View" by an open table. All validation rules in your table's properties field should also be clarified at this stage. Within the "Datasheet View." tab, those aren't available.

To proceed with, Establish an Email field if you do not own one; also, make sure your data is set to "Text, type" once an email field is required to be active.

Hit "F6" to go with Field Properties, then switch to "Validation Rule." Help make sure that certain prior changes are retained. Well, before reaching the validation guidelines, hit the "Save" key.

Paste & copy the following within that Validation Rule field: "(like "? @?.?" & "[,;]*")"

Such a string helps you format mailing addresses with characters separated by the "@" key.

Within the Validation Text, introduce the text that appears if someone forgets to enter a mailing address or types it in an inappropriate format. It will manifest itself.

"Please include a '@' mark as well as the domain name in the mailing address, e.g., 'JennyH@microsoft.com.'"

Though inserting the text within the "Validation Text" sector remains optional; it prevents a typical or ambiguous reaction from being displayed when errors occur.

Do save the work when you activate or exit "Design View" unless you make a mistake and choose to exit your view before saving. When you change views, Access prompts you to "Save."

CONCLUSION

We know your workday is hectic. Why spend hours trying to figure out Excel, when you could find the answer at the touch of a screen? You can use Excel to analyze sales transactions, stock prices, and even survey responses. It's one of the most powerful spreadsheets out there!

Microsoft Excel is a spreadsheet for Windows that helps you analyze and share data quickly and easily. Almost all of the functions you need to calculate, plot, and compare data are built right into Excel.

With more than 2 million users worldwide, Excel is the No. 1 choice among business professionals for formula-driven financial analysis and reporting.

Microsoft Excel uses a new approach to let users view their spreadsheets as PowerPoint presentations before printing or sending them as electronic files via email or Internet connection.

As we end this book, here are some more tips for you to remember to maximize your use of Microsoft Excel:

- To create a new spreadsheet, go to the "Start" menu and select "Programs," then expand the folder for your version of Excel.

- To add or delete rows or columns in your spreadsheet, go to the "Edit" menu and select "Merge and Center."
- To add a table to your spreadsheet, click on cell A1, go to the "Insert" menu and choose "Table," then follow the prompts to add specific categories and data for each category.
- When you start a new Excel document, place it on your computer's desktop to give yourself an open area in which to copy and paste cell data while you're working.
- To find the most recently used functions, go to the "Tools" menu and select "References."
- To have Excel automatically adjust your spreadsheet as you type data, click on the "Advanced" tab and select the "Automatically Refresh Cells as You Type" function.
- To show or hide a chart, click on the arrow at the bottom right of a cell, go to "Chart," and either turn off or on a chart.
- Pasting from Word is a good way to get your data into Excel. First, copy your data from Word by going to "Edit" and clicking on "Copy." Then go to Excel and paste your copied data under the "Cells" tab.
- When you click on a cell in a column, Excel automatically displays all the cells in that column whose values match the criteria you typed in.
- To access all related as functions to a specific function, click on the "Function" menu next to the function you want and select "Properties."

- To insert a graph or chart next to your data, click on cell A1, go to "Insert" and select "Chart." When you select this option, Excel inserts a vertical bar that allows you to insert your graph or chart into the document.
- If you want to save your work as a file to send via email or upload to the Internet, click on "Save As" and choose a specific location for your saved file.
- To sum up the total value of all selected cells, click on the "Tools" menu and select "Data Analysis." Then choose "Add-Ins" under the Series menu, followed by choosing Cell Name from the Categories box, followed by typing in SUM(DataCellRange) under Function 1.

I hope that this book has been a valuable tool for you. Excel definitely deserves a spot on your desktop!

www.ingramcontent.com/pod-product-compliance
Lightning Source LLC
Chambersburg PA
CBHW071139050326
40690CB00008B/1505